HR Analytics and Innovations in Workforce Planning

HR Analytics and Innovations in Workforce Planning

Dr. Tony Miller

BUSINESS EXPERT PRESS

First published in 2017 by
Business Expert Press, LLC
222 East 46th Street, New York, NY 10017
www.businessexpertpress.com

ISBN-13: 978-1-63157-622-5 (paperback)
ISBN-13: 978-1-63157-621-8 (e-book)

Business Expert Press Human Resource Management and Organizational Behavior Collection

Collection ISSN: 1946-5637 (print)
Collection ISSN: 1946-5645 (electronic)

Cover and interior design by S4Carlisle Publishing Services Private Ltd., Chennai, India

First edition: 2017

10 9 8 7 6 5 4 3 2 1

Printed in the United States of America.

*Dedicated to all Human Resource professionals worldwide
who really want to make a difference.
www.tony-miller.com*

Abstract

This book sets out new approaches, formulas, and software needed to enable any HR function or organization to forecast trends and to use existing retrospective data to their organization's advantage; which, in short, is to maximize efficiency and productivity.

You will encounter the new formulas to use and new approaches that will add value. You will find out that most of the existing 52 formulas available don't work in today's environment. There is new software that will enable you to do forecasts with certainty and you can use a new mathematical model to rightsize any organization.

Are you using an outdated organizational model? Do you have processes that don't work any more? These are areas which are major inhibitors to productivity and can be significantly improved.

Most important of all is that this book will help you to create immense added value in any organization.

Keywords

Efficiency, forecasting, HR Analytics, manpower, organizational design, productivity, profitability, rightsizing, value added, workforce planning.

Contents

Acknowledgments

To the 1000-plus HR professionals worldwide who have shared their frustrations with me about the inability to measure HR activities and who unwittingly contributed to creating the need for me to write this book.

HR software—specific to HR Analytics—is not complicated but is vital. Much of the effective software you need for creating value has been developed and fully supports many of the examples used in this book. Duncan Williamson has worked tirelessly to evolve cheap and effective programs that all run in Excel.

To the many organizations that took part in the "work done" survey so that poor performers could be categorized and their lost performance measured and costed. This vital study is the foundation to differentiation and is essential when rightsizing your organization.

Introduction

The purpose of this book is to aid existing personnel in the old-style manpower/planning department to transition into a position where they can add extra value. This is a practical book, not strictly an A–Z, is based on methodologies and processes that work in today's fast-moving and demanding environment.

If you're an academic, you will be so disappointed as many of the pillars of calculus you would expect to see are not here. This is not a treatise about mathematical reference, rather a workbook for practitioners in HR and efficiency management. Most of the applications are focused in the private sector where all results need to contribute to the bottom line. However, I see little if any difference if they were applied in the Public sector.

Reading this book will provide you with the knowledge and skills to be able to do predictive workforce planning, supported with formulas and some free downloadable software—and software advice.

CEOs and CFOs would benefit from understanding what value a modern Workforce Planning section could offer to any organization. The results are often so significant, I truly believe any New Workforce

Master Class during World HR summit

Planning department should be a profit center—and bonuses based on the amount of value created each year.

In 2016, two separate reports have both concluded that HR is one of the few professions that is set to grow significantly in the next five years. The critical area is, creating value through the human resource—New Workforce Planning will be in the vanguard of this trend.

CHAPTER 1

Manpower Planning vs Old Workforce Planning

1.1 What's the Difference Between Manpower Planning and Old Workforce Planning?

These are exciting times for HR, but we need to understand the significant change that is taking place, as organizations need to see results.

Old Manpower planning was definitely focused on retrospective data. It was also a tactical rather than a strategic tool of the business. Its prime focus seems to have evolved into producing as much retrospective management information as possible and to be able to answer all management queries relating to past manpower events. There is little evidence to support that old Manpower planning was little more than a data producer. Almost 95% of its total activities were devoted to data farming and providing information on a monthly and quarterly basis.

Looking at just some of the reporting areas of the old-style manpower planning will be enough to depress anybody. Managers, believing they were getting useful information would get vast amounts of data-ladened reports; little if any of the information contained therein was of much practical use, particularly when looking at or developing future strategic plans.

Many of the formulas used by the old-style manpower planning were based on very old formulas, and as we know now, most of those have no practical business use. I have traced over 55 such formulas and less than 10 of them have any real business benefit in today's fast-paced organizations. We must also remember that when many of these formulas were written, it was in a time before the computer revolution.

In concluding about the Old Manpower planning,

- it was tactical rather than strategic
- it used retrospective data and produced retrospective reports
- most of the formulas used were not suited for modern business
- Little evidence that specific dedicated computer programs were used.

1.2 Information Provided by Old-Style Manpower Planning. Driven by the Volume of Information Mostly Retrospective

Information on jobs.

Number of jobs.

Whether temporary/permanent/shift/day work/hour.

Department/section.

Occupation and level in organization.

Skills and education and knowledge required.

Information on people.

Number of employees.

Temporary/permanent/shift/day work/hour.

Skills and education level achieved.

Grade/salary.

Sex.

Age.

Date started (length of service).

Information on jobs.

Number of jobs.

Whether temporary/permanent/shift/day work/hour.

Department/section.

Occupation and level in organization.

Skills and education and knowledge required.

Information on people.

Number of employees.

Temporary/permanent/shift/day work/hour.

Skills and education level achieved.

Grade/salary.

Sex.

Age.

Date started (length of service).

Number of leavers.

Temporary/permanent/shift/day work/hours.

Date of leaving and length of service at leaving.

Reason for leaving.

Age on leaving.

Grade/salary.

Sex.

Education/skills.

Overtime and contractors and agency staff.

Overtime and contractors used.

Department.

Occupation.

Reason.

Number of vacancies—temporary/permanent.

Department.

Occupation and level.

Reason for vacancy—(leaver, unrequisitioned establishment, etc.).

Whether advertised or being advertised.

Whether filled by agency staff.

Length of time unfilled.

Information on recruits.

Number of recruits.

Temporary/permanent/shift/day work/hour.

Date of starting.

Age at recruitment.

Grade/salary.

Skill and education level.

Source and method of entry.

Sex.

Occupation and level in organization recruited to.

Number of promotions.

Temporary/permanent/shift/day work/hour.

Date of promotion.

Reason for promotion.

Grade/salary promoted from and to.

Skill/education level.

Sex.

Age.

Occupation and level in the organization promoted
from and to.

Length of service.

Number of employees absent.

Days lost.

Occupation and level in the organization.

Grade.

Age and Sex.

1.3   New Workforce Planning Now More Correctly Referred to as HR Analytics—Driven by Quality Information—Mainly Predictive

The future of New Workforce Planning transforms it into a specialist function. Statisticians, HR specialists, strategists, and creative types all have their place in this fast developing and most exciting function within HR. What's different—everything!

New workforce planning uses retrospective data but presents it as predictive data always accompanied by an explanation and professional advice. Specialist software is needed as new workforce planning requires sophisticated tools enabled to predict, cost, and show workforce requirements and trends in the future. What's needed for this new workforce planning?

- Strategic thinkers, not tactical personnel
- Greater use of creativity than ever before to provide innovative and competitive advantage
- Masters of predictive information with solutions
- Masters of measurement for the five indicators on the productivity dashboard
- Ability to produce information with financial implications/benefits.

- Creators of measurable added value
- 95% of the work carried out by new workforce planning is predictive
- ability to use a range of specialist software needed in new workforce planning

Critical information forecast:

Trends Age, Sickness, Organizational stability forecast

Predictions When to reorganize using the MILLER model, skill, and working pattern changes

Correlations Time off/smokers, Training/productivity, etc.

Costs Cost of recruitment, training, staff turnover, lost time, and reliability

Critical periods for Business process Re-engineering, Organizational structure Re-modeling

Strategic Planning—For short, medium, and long term. Developing plans for emergency, growth, and contraction.

Focus—using every opportunity to maximize the Human capital

New Workforce Planning requires new and innovative software, new models, and above all software that provides predictive information. It is no longer acceptable for Workforce Planners to do crude estimates or to just provide part of the solution. Organizations are demanding turnkey solutions, and we as workforce planners are in the perfect position to provide that solution.

1.4   HR Analytics/workforce planning—Where Does It Fit in HR?

Workforce Planning is not just a new term for Manpower Planning. It is a completely different way of getting the best from the human resource. It works at a strategic level, whereas old Manpower planning functioned mainly at a tactical level.

Workforce management is also referred to as human resource planning, just to complicate things. In the diagram, you will see where work (HRP) fits into the overall work of a new HR function. The activities that are carried out by workforce management are significantly different. Included in the new spectrum of responsibilities, which may come as a surprise, is business process re-engineering. It is not possible to get the best out of our human resource without having processes that are capable of being excellent in themselves. Business process re-engineering has always been like an orphan in an organization with nobody taking care of it; and when things need to change, the outcry is normally "we need consultants". By then, of course, it is normally too late and very costly.

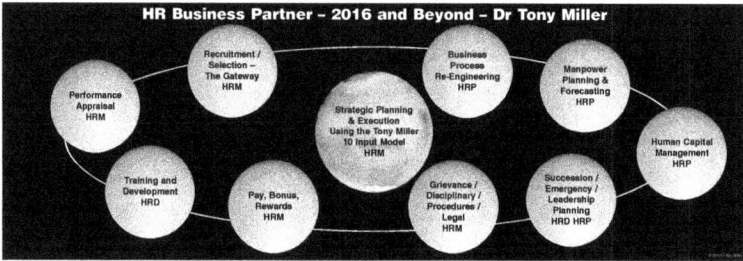

Workforce planning works best at a strategic level. When you see the full range of functions in new workforce management, it is clear that its new focus is very much strategic and its prime customers are the chief executive and the main board.

1.4.1 The Three Critical Levels

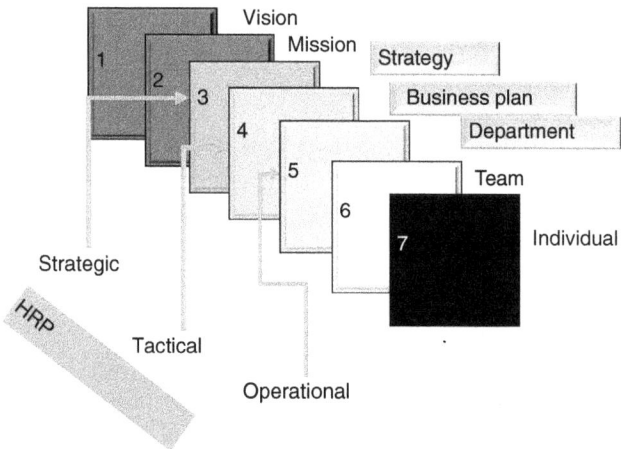

The next level is that of tactical, involving the necessary actions to execute the 1- to 3-year business plan. Workforce management can do a good job here although it is at the strategic level where it will excel.

The final level is really day-to-day management of people. Workforce management is very weak in this area as this really isn't anything to do with planning, rather correcting other people's mistakes or compensating for their bad planning. Line managers are notorious for causing havoc in this area, normally with trying to cover up their inability to make longer-term plans. Examples of this are normally recruitment issues where increased workloads or expanding business plans require extra personnel. Normally left too late, it then becomes an urgent issue to resolve—causing panic, and often very unsatisfactory implementation.

The role of workforce management is therefore best executed at the strategic level, contributing significantly to the building of the strategic plan and providing management at the most senior level with predictive information (covered later).

Best results come from working with predictive data

CHAPTER 2

Strategy and New Workforce Planning Role on the Strategic Map

2.1 Strategic Background

Strategic involvement for HR seems to be the inevitable development of this important function.

To date, many HR professionals have found increased difficulty in trying to get to grips with current HR strategic models. Most of the existing models, although well-meaning, are oversimplistic and in the main do not provide the amount of critical information needed to collect and produce high-level strategic information.

The strategic tool in this chapter is specifically focused on providing you with a complete map for not only putting together the HR strategy but ensuring full integration with the business requirements.

Before getting to grips with the map, let's just spend a moment looking at timelines for the formulation of HR strategy.

There are three timelines we need to be aware of.

First, what we can learn from previous experience looking retrospectively at what we have done.

The second strategic timeline relates to current issues and information which needs to be resolved in the future.

The third and most important timeline is that of the future. It is only the future that we really have control of. From a strategic viewpoint, it is the most important.

Often, this timeline comprises both retrospective and current issues.

Most businesses today use a model of some sort to ensure continuity and for putting strategic plans together.

The majority of these models consist of a combination of best practice in strategic planning and therefore use established strategic models such as PEST and FIVE FORCES.

In addition to those two models, specifically for New Workforce Planning there is the MILLER model which looks specifically at productivity over time.

This model is essentially an HR model but tends to be reviewed by the majority of the other strategic partners.

The MILLER model, although being a strategic HR model, is specifically aimed at detecting when organizations need to change or reinvent themselves.

Therefore, it has added importance for use in HR departments as it is HR's responsibility to point out strategically when change in the organization needs to be triggered.

The additional information not covered in the aforementioned three models is that of the strategic partners' specific area of expertise.

As well as using these strategic models, each partner will have a checklist of what to look at and report on for the future in their next strategic plan.

From what I've been told by hundreds of HR professionals internationally, this is the area that current HR professionals are having most difficulty with.

The map included here gives you a checklist of some of the most important HR areas to examine and use to see if there needs to be a specific inclusion in your strategic plan for those items.

Having worked through the checklist and drawn up your strategic plan, you can see from the map that there is then the strategic mix, HR strategy does not stand on its own.

It is part of a far more complicated strategy, as it has to integrate with the corporate strategy of all of the other business partners.

It is therefore extremely likely and from my experience, inevitable that HR strategy will need to be reworked a number of times before it is ready for full integration into the overall business strategy.

2.2   The Strategic HR Map

Our HR map shown here, may at first sight seem very complicated.

It is in three parts, Strategic Input, Strategic Output and Business Plans for Action.

You will see that all of the business partners input their strategic requirements in the form of PEST, FIVE FORCES, and their individual strategic requirements, into the strategic mix.

The latter are extremely specific to the strategic partners' own function.

On the map you will notice that we have highlighted the areas that are the specific function of the human resources professional.

We hope that this will help you with the requirements needed to formulate your human resources strategic plan.

The specific input for human resources into the strategic plan takes the form of the 10 indicators.

These 10 subject headings provide a sound basis for the organization input needed from human resources. The 10 subject headings provide the initial human resources input for the first part of the strategic input. It will become obvious when studying the map that New Workforce Planning has a major contribution to the overall HR strategy, being actively involved in the majority of strategic inputs.

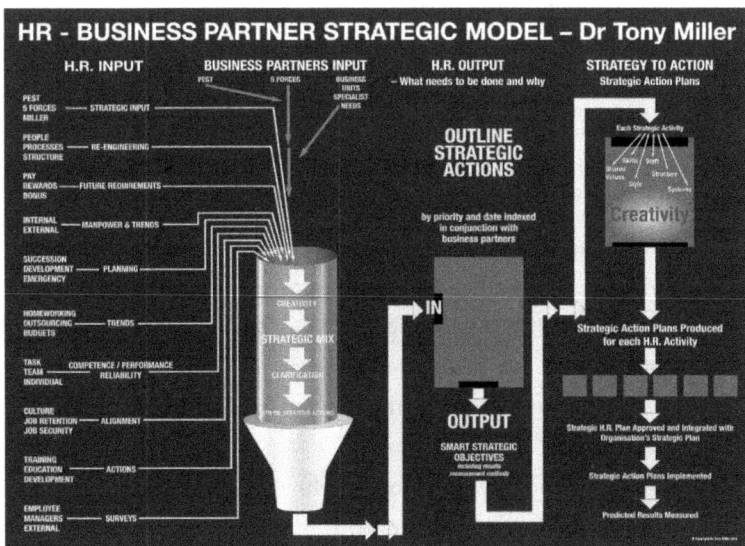

2.3   HR—The 10 Critical Inputs

1. **Strategic Input**—this consists all three strategic models, PEST, FIVE FORCES, and MILLER organizational maturity model

    a. PEST—The PEST analysis is a long-range tool. It is used to identify: Political/legal issues

    Economic

    Social trends and changes

    Technology—innovations and change

    b. FIVE FORCES

    Competition among existing firms

    The threat of new entrants

    The threat of substitute products or services

    Bargaining power of customers

    Bargaining power of suppliers

    c. MILLER organizational change model

    The MILLER model looks at organizational productivity over time.

    Because organizations grow and productivity increases with time, this happens up to a point, after which the organization goes into decline. At that point, the organization typically employs too many people, is too procedure-bound and does not produce enough output. This is rather similar to a product bell curve.

    The position of the organization or department is found by using a questionnaire, which gives a plot on the MILLER curve. The questionnaire is included in this book; Appendix 3, for you to use.

2. **Re-engineering**

    What HR processes need to be changed—what will be necessary and what will be the impact.

    What HR actions in the strategic plan there that might require process change, what are they and what their impact is.

    Will the re-engineering impact on any of the following?

    PEOPLE—will we need to change the organization numbers of people we employ to fit the new process? What is the value of the saving?

    PROCESS—the physical process. How we implement the process change and how it will be carried out. What is its value?

STRUCTURE—organizational structure needed to support re-engineering and either people, process or changes brought about by the indicators in the MILLER model

3. **Future Requirements**

PAY—what pay levels are likely to be in the market place? What do we need to do? What are the financial projections?

REWARDS—is the allowance and benefits scheme competitive, what actions are needed to change?

What is the cost and the real value to the individual and the organization? Would rewards be better consolidated into either higher pay or bigger bonus schemes?

BONUS—projected cost. Is the scheme right for our business—are we getting the productivity we need? If the bonus scheme is to be changed then what is the cost, projected productivity improvement and an indication of our position against our direct competitors?

4. **Manpower and Trends**—These need to be predictive trends which will cover things such as sickness, inclusion, productivity, demographic, skills shortages, turnover, longevity in employment, speed to competency, organizational shape

5. **Planning**

SUCCESSION—key personnel succession plans, desirable succession plans

DEVELOPMENT—trend/cost—speed competence, speed to performance, training needs

EMERGENCY—contingency plans for people in an organizational emergency, involvement of retired people, universities, other resources

6. **Trends**

HOME WORKING—what are the current trends and how they will impact on organizational structure, pay and conditions and productivity?

OUTSOURCING – identification of areas of the business, activities and processes which could be outsourced. ROI and organizational implications

BUDGETS—forecasting for HR budgetary requirements to meet strategic objectives for manpower.

To include salary, training, allowances, and bonus payments.

7. **Competence Performance and Reliability (explained further in Chapter 8)**

   TASK—business performance trends via a Monte Carlo simulation, staff turnover, project approach impact on productivity, initiatives to improve productivity, competent trends projected, competency strengths and weaknesses by department.

   INDIVIDUAL—competency/performance trends and reliability

   TEAM—introduction/expansion of teams/team types and productivity projected gains and reporting and providing on the productivity dashboard

8. **Alignment**

   CULTURE—progress with the alignment of the corporate culture template will stop suggested actions/amendments needed depending on the suggested strategic objectives and the final strategic requirements.

   JOB RETENTION—effects of job retention in the future, market trends, change in organizational shape, use of talented development techniques.

   JOB SECURITY – techniques needed to give employees security and connectivity with the organization. May include share/stock options, development programs, long-term contracts.

9. **Actions**

   TRAINING—training budget required for future, ROI on training, training efficiency relating to productivity. Training efficiency relating to competencies. External and internal trends on training.

   EDUCATION—educational standards required for the future, need to invest in education and second degrees. Link between educational standards and performance at work.

   DEVELOPMENT—career development needed for the company. Internal and external trends in development. Development strategies for succession planning within the company.

ROI figures for development effectiveness

10. **Surveys**

EMPLOYEE—satisfaction surveys relating to be linked between current state and future state of the corporate culture.

MANAGERS—surveys with the managers of the company to check cultural alignment and satisfaction with the working environment in the company.

Any actions which may be necessary to take for the future.

As you can see, New Workforce Planning has a direct input into 6 of the 10 strategies: 1,2,4,5,6,7 refers.

2.4   The Strategic Mix

The next stage is where the business provides its requirements (Business Partners Input) and during consultative meetings the HR strategic plan needs to be put into alignment with the overall business requirements and needs to reflect a total picture of what is required.

This approach avoids the embarrassment of HR going to the strategic table with no ideas and nothing to offer. It also clearly shows the business that HR is being a clear strategic thinker and able to devise and propose strategies which are truly strategic.

This map has only been in existence for a short while and already HR managers are reporting that other areas of the business are keen to draw up identical maps showing their specific strategic inputs.

2.4.1 Strategic Approval

Once the strategic blend has been completed final plans can be made and submitted for approval. Once approved the task of turning strategy into action commences.

2.5   Strategy into Action

There are a number of ways this can be done. Using the 6 S model seems to work best for human resource strategic plans.

Each HR strategic action will need to be translated into a strategic action plan with what resource and cost.

These plans can all be integrated into a comprehensive HR business plan for the short, medium, and long term.

Constructing HR strategic action plans gives you the perfect tool to upload all of the plans into one integrated process using something like Microsoft Project Manager.

The entire strategic plan of the business can then be run and operated as a major project with all the discipline of a major project.

2.5.1 The Role of Creativity

Specifically referred to twice on the strategic map, creativity needs to excel during strategic planning.

The whole process of the strategy gives us a unique opportunity to be creative in the way that would write and carry out our strategic plans.

Competitive advantage certainly will not be achieved by copying or following what we have done in the past.

In such a fast-changing world, we should focus our attention very much on improvement, or, what is more exciting, doing things completely differently.

A very simple idea to follow is the FACE approach not only to internal customers but also external customers. First used by Dr Michael Hammer, this is very useful for focusing the mind.

The face principle requires us to deliver processes and concepts that meet its requirements.

These are:

Fast

Accurate

Cheap

Easy

In addition, I am reminded of Peter Drucker's advice to always ask the question "Would the roof cave in if we stopped doing this altogether"?

We must make sure as a strategic partner that we do not create processes or activities which significantly take energy away from the business.

That means radically re-examining lot of processes and trying to either abolish them or modify them so as not to take up valuable human capital time and effort. Our quest as HR professionals must be to energize and focus the Human Capital to maximize its potential and therefore achieve significant competitive advantage. Effective and creative strategic processes are a major step in the right direction.

2.6   Writing Strategic Action Plans

The 6 S model

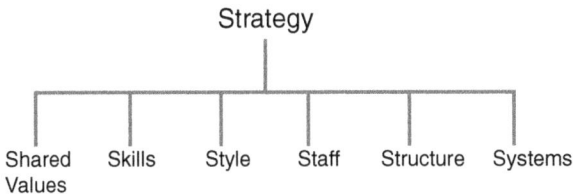

The framework used here is the Miller/Sporlein model. This was developed by the author and a German Manager and was a significant modification of the McKinsey 7's framework. In that framework, organizational actions or outcomes were divided into seven categories—each as important as the other. The key to success was ensuring all of the component parts were effectively achieving or contributing to the overall goals.

The Miller/Sporlein model suggested that the key driver would always be the strategy which therefore drives or influences the six subsequent S's.

The framework looks as follows:

The "driver"—the "strategy"—is self-explanatory. The other tables used are as follows:

Shared Values—This is the culture of the company. The invisible glue of values and beliefs that bond the organization.

Skills—The skills needed to carry out any new strategy. These skills may be needed by your staff or may have to be imported via consultants for a special project.

Style—The management style needed to ensure that the strategy is implemented. This needs to be in harmony with the requirements of the shared values.

Staff—Have you sufficient, too many, right caliber, etc.?

Structure—Is the structure of the organization correct to carry out the needs of the strategy?

Systems–Will the existing systems (computer) and processes support the requirements that the previous six S's will demand?

From a BUSINESS PROFESSIONAL'S perspective, there are points of focus for compiling a Company Strategy.

1. PAST—Designing strategies to rectify existing company problems of shortfalls.
2. PRESENT—Designing strategies that are strategic enablers for others' strategic ideas.
3. FUTURE—Compiling strategies that are proactive and will provide proactive added value.

Whatever the strategic aims, using a framework to explore all the possibilities is a process that will give structure to your thoughts for the strategic plan and the resulting operations plan/budget that is needed.

Having used the strategic framework, the ideas can be worked on and the plan produced. The underlying thoughts when producing your input should be 'Is this really added value?' and 'How will I measure the success of my work?'

There needs to be liaison with all the key players when strategic plans are produced.

This simple model is worth remembering when doing any of your strategic planning. It's easy to find expensive solutions to everything, the trick is to spend a minimum amount, cause the minimum disruption and get the maximum effort.

Triple W Objective Setting [©] This system was designed by Dr. Tony Miller. Recognizing that managers and supervisors just did not get SMART objectives he used knowledge from his strategic mapping process to come up with triple W objective setting.

Using the 6 S methodology

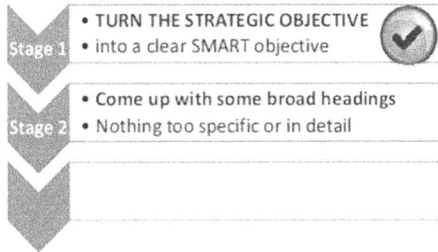

- **TURN THE STRATEGIC OBJECTIVE**
- into a clear SMART objective

Stage 1

- **Come up with some broad headings**
- Nothing too specific or in detail

Stage 2

Using the 6 S methodology

- **TURN THE STRATEGIC OBJECTIVE**
- into a clear SMART objective

Stage 1

- **Come up with some broad headings**
- Nothing too specific or in detail

Stage 2

- **Involve the "how" people now**
- Get things done via SAP's

2.6.1 The Basic Concept

Most objectives are a result of strategic requirements and strategy focuses on three main areas, What needs to be done, Why it needs to be done and finally When it needs to be done by. That applied and you get all you need to set very clear and easy to understand objectives.

2.6.2 The Process

The first **W** is the **What**, what is it that needs to be done, or what is it that needs doing.

This needs to be spelt out so that it's clear to understand.

So let's practice:

To improve productivity in the back office by 20% this year (that's before the triple W process).

What Is Required:

- *To increase the number of case files dealt with by 20% a month, that's 50 extra, 600 extra in a year*

- *The work is to be locked into a project program on our Microsoft office management system showing all the deliverable dates and number of extra files processed – the exact numbers to be show for each month.*

Why: Without the why, the person doing the objective will never fully understand the context of their

objective and why, if they have this information they may be able to produce a better way of doing it.

- *In order for our company to be competitive we must increase our volume but without incurring any extra costs, such as more manpower.*
- *The timing will be crucial as the sales force have very specific targets to achieve and this will directly affect our workload commencing on the 1st October this year. Everyone should be aware this is a priority as it is a key element of our strategy.*

Finally, the When: It is critical here to be specific. Don't just give an end date. Anyone who has managed projects will tell you that that's asking for slippage. So take time to break the objective into manageable chunks. Dates given should be by day, month and year. Where figures are involved, try not to use percentages but exact numbers – this will avoid confusion or any misunderstanding.

- *This objective fits in with the department strategy to continuous improvement and innovation by demonstrating its efficiency improvements over the next 5 years.*
- *The plan for achieving this is required for outline approval by the 2nd April 2015 and must be agreed and approved by 1st May 2015*
- *The first batch increase is needed by 1st October 2015 (50 files) and the total objective is to be completed showing the 600 extra files by 1st October 2016*

One of the greatest assists to performance improvement to any business is using this system to ensure thing get done on time and within budget.

Managers and supervisors only require a short but focused piece of training to be able to do this—remember that there is a vast difference between the managers saying they can do it and the reality of well-written Objectives.

You may be wondering in the Triple W objective method why there is no explanation of how to do it. With today's workforce, people are bright enough to work this out themselves or to find out. If they take the objective on board and work out how to do it, then they will be more committed and accountable for the outcome as it's their idea. This simple but effective approach really does produce results and more importantly gets a lot more commitment to action.

2.6.3 Background to Strategic Action Plans

An important document to ensure that projects are well-defined, focused, and most importantly meets organizational requirements. The strategic action plan states:

- What is to be achieved
- What will be covered
- A plan of how and when each item is to be delivered
- Risks that might be associated with delivery
- Dependencies—who you are dependent upon to make things happen

An important aspect of the document is that it is in a standard format and needs approving both prior to and after delivery ensuring that the end customer or sponsor gets exactly what they are expecting.

Each part of the project needs a Strategic action plan and each has its own Strategic action plan project manager.

Timing—A first cut of the Strategic action Plan is to be ready by . . .

Sponsor—The customer/sponsor for each of Strategic action Plans (that's you)

Methodology—Initially, all concerned will produce their own project plans and time lines.

Help on construction of the plans can be sought from . . . .

When completing the strategic action plan, it is important to stick to a standard methodology as all strategic action plans will need to be integrated eventually.

Front Cover

- Quality Plan for "project name"
- Project Manager
- Version
- Version Date
- Date Approved

(Note: The version numbers should be in decimal points until approval. When this is determined then it becomes version 1.)

2.6.3.1 Scope

What the plan is going to achieve, what will be covered and also what is excluded?

2.6.3.2 Deliverables

Each project will have a number of tasks, which together provide the components for the total project. Each manageable task or group of tasks will make up one of the project deliverables. In this section of the Quality Plan it is essential that all of the deliverables are identified. When you have a team of people working on your project you will need to assign certain deliverables to the appropriate person.

2.6.3.3 Plan

The deliverables need to be translated to timelines so that the Strategic Action plan can be tracked together with all the other plans and activities during the project.

2.6.3.4 Risks

As with any project there may be risks, which unless addressed will adversely affect either the quality or timelines of the project. These need to be clearly identified so they can be addressed.

2.6.3.5 Dependencies

Certain areas of your project will be dependent on other people in the organization helping you. It may be that there is a specific action needed before you can action certain critical tasks—these need to be included in the plan.

2.6.3.6 Sign On

The Customer/Sponsor will sign the Strategic action plans collectively. This will happen when he is sure all the elements are in place and that the total plans provide the Solution.

2.6.3.7 Sign Off

Once the project is complete the Customer/Sponsor will sign off the documentation only when all the deliverables have been delivered to the agreed specification.

2.6.4 Strategic Action Plan—Example

Training needed for new working procedures and software
Project Manager:
Russ Edell

Version   .10

Version Date   5-22-15
Date Approved _____

2.6.5 Scope

To develop, test and deliver a training program for new loan counselors, processors, their team leaders and Finet Direct managers. To create corporate awareness through the training of Finet customer suppliers and their staff (vision only).

2.6.6 This Training Program Will be Directed Toward Four Major Product Areas

1. 30/15-year fixed conforming loans (and all other Desktop Originator products).
2. 30/15-year FHA loans
3. 30/15-year VA loans
4. Equity lines of credit

Excluded from this Strategic action plan is the training of support personnel. A training program for these positions may be developed at a later time depending on needs yet to be determined.

2.6.7 Deliverables

The overall objective is to produce a training program that will train existing and new loan counselors, loan processors and their leaders to staff the best call center in the world.

1. Design and build a training facility with the following attributes:
   a. 13 workstations—12 for trainees, 1 for instructor. Workstations will be identical to workstations
   In the call center, both in hardware and software, but under no circumstances will they access the call center programs. (Exact specifications to be provided by the Systems Strategic action plan.) In addition, a number of high-tech items will be required to enhance the training.
   b. The training facility needs an open area in addition to the workstation area, to facilitate non-computer group training.   MIS 7-25-15
2. Record existing Loan Counselor/Customer conversations for review by Performance Advantage. RE 5-23-15
3. Complete a need analysis to define the requirements of some of the training blocks. As of this time the projected training blocks would be:
   a. Finet culture and team building
   b. Relationship selling

    c. Product knowledge for 30-year fixed conforming loans and all other Desktop Originator Products.

    d. Telephone usage and predictive language

    e. Team leadership and coaching techniques

    f. Putting it all together "One day in the life of a call center".
       RE 5-23-15

4. Complete a need analysis to define the requirements of the software training blocks. As of this time, the projected training blocks would be:

    a. Use of POINT software

    b. Use of DESKTOP ORIGINATOR software

    c. Use of LOAN PROSPECTOR software

    d. Help/script pop-up screen utilization

    e. Product underwriting guidelines   RE 7-12-15

5. Set up Terms of Reference (measurement requirements)

(For example)

    1. Total calls vs. total sales

    2. Letters of praise

    3. Phone matrix

    4. Competency matrix

    5. Referrals RE 6-6-15

    6. Define Core skills

(For example)

Point software

Desktop Originator software

Loan Prospector software

Telephone usage and predictive language

Accuracy of documentation

Product knowledge   RE 6-27-15

    7. Investigate the use of Brightware software for use in the Service Center.   RE 7-3-15

    8. Develop a total training program with specific objectives and phases to insure that at the completion of training the loan counselors, loan processors, and their leaders and managers will obtain a basic designated performance level based on the terms of reference and core skills.

RE 7-25-15

9. Develop lesson plans and a testing program to cover the content developed in the training program.   RE 8-8-15

10. Test the training program in a remedial mode using the existing staff.   RE 8-15-15

11. Revise the training program based on feedback received from the existing staff.   RE 8-29-15

12. Test the revised training program using the appropriate people   RE 8-21-15

13. Recruit the first class of 12 trainees.   RE 9-4-15

14. Train the first group of potential team leaders.   RE 9-19-15

15. Train the first class of 12 trainees with the participation of the team leaders.   RE 9-26-15

16. Develop training modules for other product areas, FHA VA and equity lines.   RE 10-5-15

17. Use portions of the above training modules to articulate the vision of Finet to Finet managers, Finet customer suppliers and their staff.

18. Implement the use of video, CD-ROM and other high-tech training enhancements.

19. Train other individuals to deliver training when needed.

2.6.8 Risks

1. An adequate training facility may not be available, which would greatly reduce training efficiency.

2. Point software may be so primitive and user-unfriendly that it intimidates and discourages the new trainee making it impossible to achieve the desired goals.

3. Technology group is unable or unwilling to provide the support necessary to set up help/script pop up screens in the required time frame.

4. Technology group is unable or unwilling to provide the support necessary to set up product underwriting criteria screens in the required time frame.

5. There are not enough qualified potential team leaders

2.6.9 *Dependencies*

1. Need the technology group to approve specifications and set up computer portion of training facility.
2. Need the technology group to design and implement help/script pop-up screens and timing flags (wake-up calls).
3. Need the technology group to design and implement underwriting criteria screens.
4. Need the technology group to set up phone system to record existing Loan Counselor/customer conversations to be used by Performance Advantage in Predictive Language study.
5. Need Performance Advantage to analyze existing Loan Counselor/Customer conversations using Predictive Language techniques to develop the content for help/script pop-up screens.
6. Need Dr. Tony to provide recruitment policy and procedures.
7. Need Dr. Tony to provide Loan Counselor and Team Leader salary and remuneration policy and procedures.
8. Need Nick to provide content for parts of the training.
9. Need Peggy Ann to develop the content for Product underwriting guideline screens.
10. Need Peggy Ann to provide product knowledge information.
11. Need Sara/Dr. Tony to provide Russ with Predictive Language training.
12. Need Dr. Tony to provide a cultural template for use in the development of the training program.
13. Need the CEO to provide the vision portion of the training at the beginning of each training session.
14. Need the team leaders to participate in the trainees' training.

Signed for Implementation   _____   _____

Nick Steinmetz VP Sales   *Date*

Approved by   _____   _____

Jan Hoeffel CEO   *Date*

Approved by   _____   _____

Wayne Repich COO   *Date*

Signed for Completion   _____   _____

Nick Steinmetz, VP Sales   *Date*

2.7   This Process Really Works

This end to end process really works. When used by HR it quickly becomes the norm and adopted by others areas of the business. Displaying the chart (free from the website) provides a signal to all that you have a process with is easy to follow and clearly shows the input that HR has as a strategic partner.

When actioning strategic plans the methodology shown in this chapter suits our purposes. Very often we must get things done through others in the organization and those people do not work directly for us, the strategic action plans get everyone on the same page and the project plan which is made from the 6 S model helps to keep everyone on track.

Some companies have used this technique for use at performance appraisal when objective setting.

CHAPTER 3

Organizational Design and Supervisory Ratios

3.1   Symmetrical Design

There are three types of organizational structure

- Symmetrical
- Asymmetrical
- Peoplecentric

3.1.1 Symmetrical

It was in 1760 that Adam Smith set out the ideas that would shape businesses. He made the first symmetrical designs for how an organization should look and designed the first modern organizational structure; it was first used in 1771 by a company called Arkright in Cromford in the United Kingdom. This was then adopted by a factory called Smedley in 1784 which is still functioning—officially known as the world's oldest factory.

Then adopted as the model for success by other companies worldwide, surprisingly this structure for organizations is still very much in evidence today.

Smith was also responsible for the new business titles of Supervisor and Manager and for the recommendation that the ideal span of management would be 1:7. This was appropriate in 1760 and proved to be a world-class model adopted by most of the industrial countries in the world.

Unfortunately and despite the technological and education revolution, there is still a belief that people require close supervision and must be managed.

These two factors, old organizational design and 1760 supervision have condemned us to the productivity and efficiency problems we have today. So why do so many managers and supervisors still want small ratios of control? The reason is that it's less work for them and requires less skill; but it then begs the business question—what do we pay managers for? It is estimated that 95 percent of existing businesses are still structured on the design principles of 1760 and the pioneering work of Adam Smith.

Spans of Control and Organizational Shape

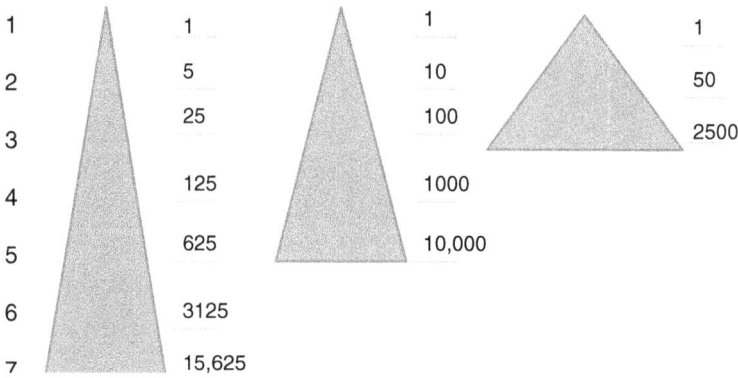

1	1	1
2	5	10
3	25	100
4	125	1000
5	625	10,000
6	3125	
7	15,625	

1	1
	50
	2500

3.2   Asymmetrical Organizations

The Asymmetrical principle does not stick to the same ratios of supervision to employee, but has different ratios for different levels and parts of the business, depending on the role, capability, and type of work undertaken. It's a much better and commonsense approach to organizational design and will always work where the organization employs smart people. It is difficult to pinpoint when this design first became used, but I guess it was probably in the late 1960s. The design has many advantages as it allows parts of the organization to have a very flat structure, while other parts are more in line with a Smith-type setup.

Above the top tier for an asymmetrical organization

Asymmetrical organization is best typified by flat organizational structures where in some cases the majority of the organization is only three to four tiers deep.

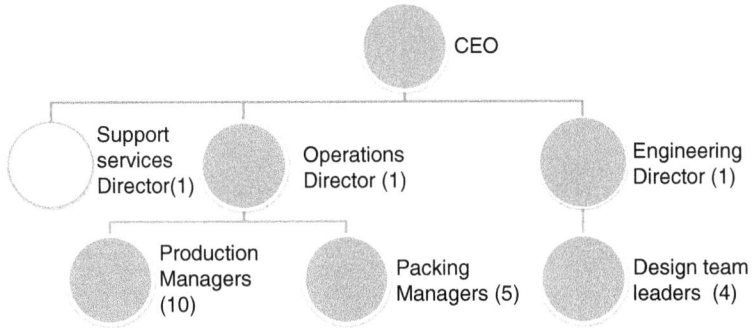

Change the structure, and change the results from this (symmetrical) to this (asymmetrical)

Benefits
- 28 percent improvement in productivity
- Less management
- Improved worker satisfaction scores

Director

Teams managers (50) each with 5 teams of 10

team of 10   team of 10   team of 10   team of 10   team of 10

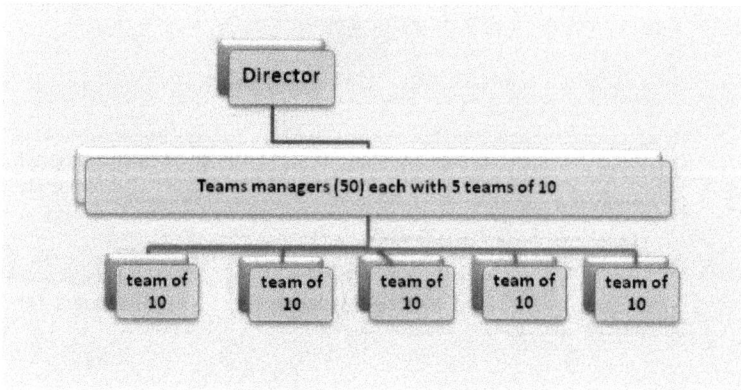

3.3   Peoplecentric Organizations

It's hard to believe that the founders of a people centric organization were all connected with the IT business and were nearly all scientists or IT engineers. Although the design is not new, the term *peoplecentric organization* was first coined by Dr. Miller at the Balkans HR summit in 2012.

The start of the peoplecentric organization happened perhaps by chance and was a spin-off of the way William Skockley worked. Shockley was simply a brilliant man. He has been credited with the revolutionary work on the transistor and later advancing semiconductors. Shockley co-invented the transistor, for which he was awarded the 1956 Nobel Prize in Physics.

Shockley's attempts to commercialize a new transistor design in the 1950s and 1960s led to California's "Silicon Valley" becoming a hotbed of electronics innovation. In his later life, Shockley was a professor at Stanford. Thus, over the course of just 20 years, a mere eight of Shockley's former employees who formed Fairchild semiconductors (named after its financier Sherman Fairchild) in Silicon Valley California later gave forth 65 new enterprises, which then went on to do the same. Shockley Semiconductor and these companies formed the nucleus of what became Silicon Valley, which revolutionized the world of electronics and, indeed, the world itself.

What Shockley had started was a new way of doing things and a new way of running efficient organizations based on a peoplecentric design; whether this was a design formed by analysis or by need we will never know—but the success of Silicon Valley speaks for itself.

The founding companies using this form of organizational design

- Shockley Transistors 1950s
- Fairchild semiconductors 1957
- Intel 1968—founded by Robert Noyce and Gordon Moore, perhaps the first company to offer stock options to all its employees and have the flat organization as we know it today
- Microsoft 1981
- Apple 1997
- Google 1998
- Facebook 2004

The peoplecentric organization is so different and is based on the concept that the organization should be designed and structured to get the best from the type of people it employs instead of designing a typical organization either symmetrical or asymmetrical and making the people fit the organization. If you are wondering if this works—take a look at the stock value of the companies mentioned.

The epitome of this design is Google. The organization was created to support those that would work in it—right from the start. The design was specific to meet the personality profile of Technological Engineers. What

Peoplecentric

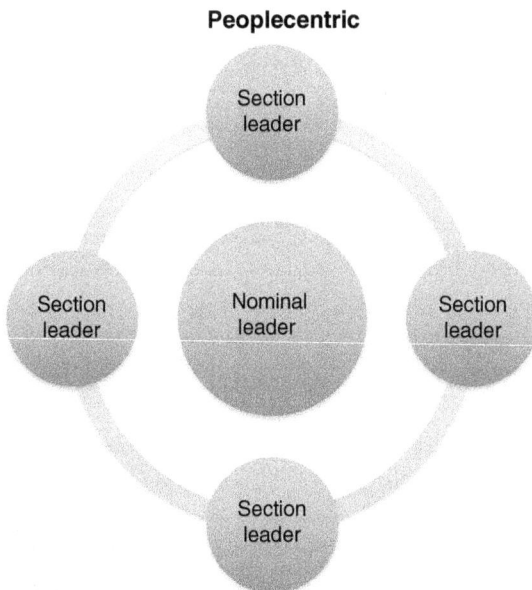

a change; instead of getting people to fit an organizational design, first deciding what people you needed (by profile) and then creating an entire organization to support that ethos. The design first became apparent in 2001 with the appointment of Eric Smitt as the new CEO. Google has always been good at recruitment (a lesson we should learn from) they had always valued people with high SAT scores and high grades from the best colleges and universities. You can't graft on mental horsepower so it's best to make sure you get it when you recruit.

The new Google organization had been created new, different, very functional and almost free of bureaucratic rules which are endemic in symmetrical organizations—the skeptics of course said it would never work—just look at the track record of Google. This design innovation was quick to be copied by Apple although the world at large has failed to capitalize on this type of organizational innovation.

The future of organizational design will become a combination of asymmetric and peoplecentric designers, when re-engineering existing organizations will be subjected to a hard time, as all the existing managers will fight the change as the day of the conventional manager being essential has now reached a plateau. Many managers realize that their days are numbered and soon their numbers will inevitably decline.

When designing the organization or re-designing an existing organization, remember that today people are educated to a very high standard; overmanage them, and you will never see them reach their potential. Overmanaged people often find work boring and this creates a disconnect between the management and the workforce. This will become very apparent and will work against the organization if for any reason the organization has to change quickly.

To conclude—be bold with the organizational design, try not to use the past as a benchmark, the greatest strengths organizations have is the untapped potential of the employees—use the organizational design to capitalize on this.

3.4   Ratios of Management

Supervisory and management ratios

As with organizational design, it was Adam Smith who first set out the ideas of how people should be managed. Please remember that back in that time, in 1760, the majority of the agricultural workforce were illiterate. Many have spent their lives in agricultural work and the start of the Industrial Revolution made a change to a new type of occupation and a very different way of working. Although it's hard to imagine it now, at that time it must have been very stressful. Days of toiling in the fields doing simple repetitive work was rapidly replaced by factory work, governed by strict timekeeping and output.

Smith's ideas were first adopted by a company called Arkwright based in Cromford in the UK. The workforce had to be managed and two new jobs were created. The first, was that of a *supervisor*. As the name suggested it was somebody who had super-vision. The supervisor in those days was only marginally brighter than the persons whom they were supervising and the job primarily, was to watch the workers and make sure they didn't wander off and were kept fully engaged at their place of work. The ratio at that time was the famous 1:7. As the supervisors were neither that reliable, nor that clever, they needed to be watched as well, and so a new job was invented—that of a *manager*. The manager's job was to watch the supervisors and to make sure that the supervisors did what they were supposed to do. As there were so many managers, it was necessary then to have a senior manager to manage the managers, and so on and so forth. This was how the organization was created and management ratios established.

It is amazing how little progress was made between 1771 and 1980. During this period there was only a slight improvement in supervisory ratios from 1:7 to 1:8. The big changes happened in the 1990s. With the worldwide introduction of the Internet, better school and university education we suddenly had a far more intelligent workforce. Supervisory ratios throughout the organization started to change and we started to see companies operating at 1:15, 1:20 and in the late 1990s some companies with ratios of 1:50. All of this is made possible by a continually improving intelligent and better informed workforce.

Gone were the days of only getting information from your line manager or supervisor, the Internet had revolutionized the way that we learn and access information. As the World Wide Web provided a learning tool for everybody, so the universal use of television widened people's horizons internationally.

The world is now (more or less) stable and the global economy is fully established. The world has become one enormous supermarket. The breaking down of international barriers for travel has meant we have seen a mass mobilization of workforces on a truly international scale

With such a well-educated international workforce, we must ask the question "have we maximized the organization in terms of how people are managed?" For the majority of the organizations, the answer must be "no!"

This is an area where workforce planning must excel and if you're looking to get strategic advantage then the whole area of how people are supervised and managed needs to change. There is an interesting correlation between intelligence and supervision. Intelligent people seem to need little if any supervision whereas poorly educated people seem to be little better than their forebears back in 1771. The only thought you need to give this is whether you are dealing with predominantly stupid people in the organization or whether you have recruited and maximized on getting the best of the best. If the latter is the case, then you have every possibility of making a substantial contribution to improving organizational efficiency and at the same time maximizing employee satisfaction with the work that they do.

As I have indicated before, the manager and that type of role has really reached its zenith, and that was in the late 1990s, the role has been replaced by that of the inspirational leader. Although these sound like very fancy words, they really are two different jobs both of which can be allocated to a specific time in history. Before the 1990s, then it was 100 percent of the domain of the manager; since the year 2014, the real requirement in successful organizations is to recruit and retain leaders at the five key levels in the organization.

Practical examples of people who I have met and have excelled at each of the five levels are as follows:

John Simpson (5)—Anglian Water was faced with the need for massive change and to prepare itself for the rigors of privatization. John Simpson was the director of operations and systematically went about changing the organization. Numbers were reduced from 6500 to 4500 with an increase

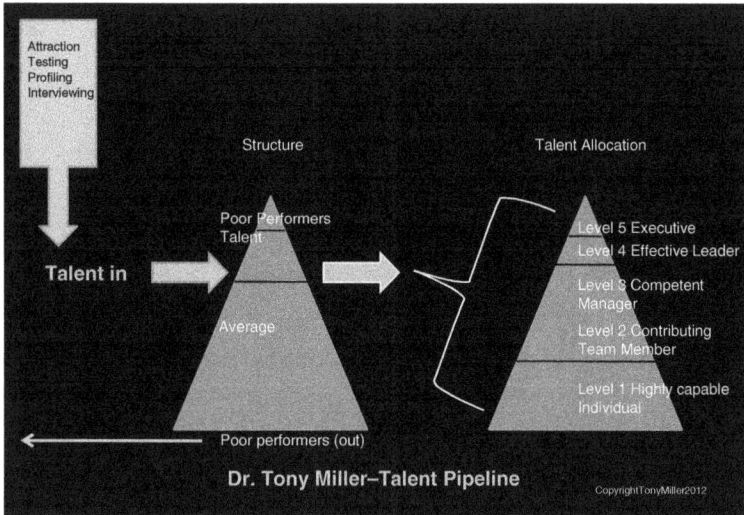

in productivity. The second major achievement was to reengineer the entire way that water operations were carried out. He led a team which carried this out in a very short period of time and the project was delivered on time. He was incredibly popular with those who are hard workers and were expert in the field operation. Poor performers feared and resented his success.

Ray Kressinger (4)—Frizzell Financial Services faced the challenge of a new competitor in the market place. Ray Kressinger was instrumental in leading a program to empower both sales and service people and his actions were instrumental in ensuring that company's long-term survival and profitability. Throughout the change he had received stiff opposition from some of the established managers in the organization and had persevered and triumphed showing an outstanding level of resilience.

Mike Jago (4)—Mike was a manager in Toshiba and took on a leading role in improving Toshiba's quality, and staff turnover problem in the UK facility. Mike showed exceptional leadership skills and quickly convinced management of the need to change by demonstrating by actions rather than words what could be achieved using different methods of working and organizing the workforce.

Paul Lewis (3)—production manager at Land Rover. Paul was instrumental in making self-managed teams work and also helped Land Rover to reduce their production line costs and in doing so established a way of work that enabled quality to increase while at the same time reduce costs. During this period staff surveys carried out by the company found that the attitude to the Company had completely changed from that of a negative consensus to one of the very positive consensus. Under Paul Lewis's stewardship, the "Freelander" was produced and the success of that vehicle needs no further words from me.

Louise Johnson (2)—work and the project officer during her time of the merger of two companies. Although at a nonmanagerial level in the company, Louise demonstrated an exceptional high level of skill and organization and consistently produced a very high level of results often requiring her to work long hours normally in very difficult circumstances with very little traditional supervision.

Shellie Musker (1)—A sales person in a large call center. Shellie took it upon herself to get training to improve her sales techniques. Shortly after her training, which was done out of office hours, she became the best sales person in the call center and remained the best for just over 1 year; she was beaten for just 1 month and then went on to produce the highest sales ever, selling twice that of average performers.

3.4.1 Performance Through Team Working

This is not new, but it is an important factor for getting good performance.
Team working and using self-managing teams is another tool to aid in maximizing organizational efficiency and getting competitive advantage. Depending on how far you want to go then you can establish an

organizational design which becomes team based. Empowered teams and self-managed teams give between 15 and 20 percent improvements in productivity normally with a relatively unchanged headcount. Type of teams and appropriate ratios are as follows:

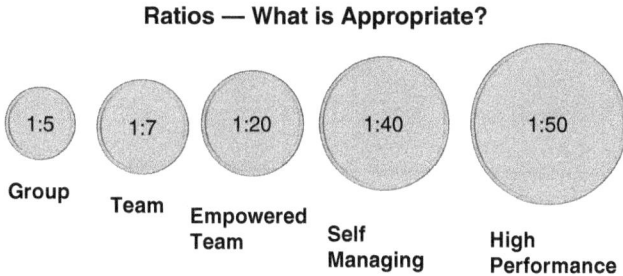

Ratios — What is Appropriate?

1:5	1:7	1:20	1:40	1:50
Group	Team	Empowered Team	Self Managing	High Performance

Team Productivity Model

You need to decide the ratio based on your business and on how brave you want to be. Once you go past empowered teams, there is very little need for managers—they are best replaced with team or department leaders, but in noticeably smaller numbers. When doing this exercise, be wary of people pressurizing you to have leaders and deputies in the team—you really don't need them, the same with the rest of the structure. My motto is always to do an ironing board design—flat and simple.

It's also a good policy not to chase the numbers of staff, getting the design right is the key issue and the numbers needed tend then to become self-evident.

The model that works well here when looking at bonus and rewards is the Adair model

- Teams need to be task focused in order to get the best from them
- Teams need rewarding for outstanding team performance using something like a hopper bonus scheme referred to in my book *New HR*
- Finally, every organization is a combination of individuals. For outstanding contribution—individuals need recognition.

Pay and bonus schemes are not normally within the domain of workforce planning, which is a pity as it would, from an organizational point of view, provide a complete service from design of systems, assessing people through to performance management of your human resource. This is yet another example of the lack of joined-up thinking that still is evident in many HR functions today.

3.5   Downsizing

Downsizing is a term used in workforce planning for altering significantly the structure of the organization. Normally it is done to both symmetrical and asymmetrical organization at a period (mid-stage two) in the MILLER organizational maturity chart. Downsizing is a risky business as it involved taking out complete layers of management. Downsizing is normally but not always preceded by doing business process re-engineering.

The key to successful downsizing is to remove layers of management in the organization by finding out the answer to one simple question:

Where in the organization is the work actually done?

Although the question sounds simple—it's often not that easy to find the organization. Every layer claiming, "this is where the work is done."

Organization before delayering (operations functions only) U.K.

Once you have established the truth, then you can go about removing the layers and completely restructuring the organization by delayering.

Organization after downsizing FS U.K.

Benefits
- 28 percent improvement in productivity
- Less management
- Improved worker satisfaction scores

Although there are so many examples of this, recently

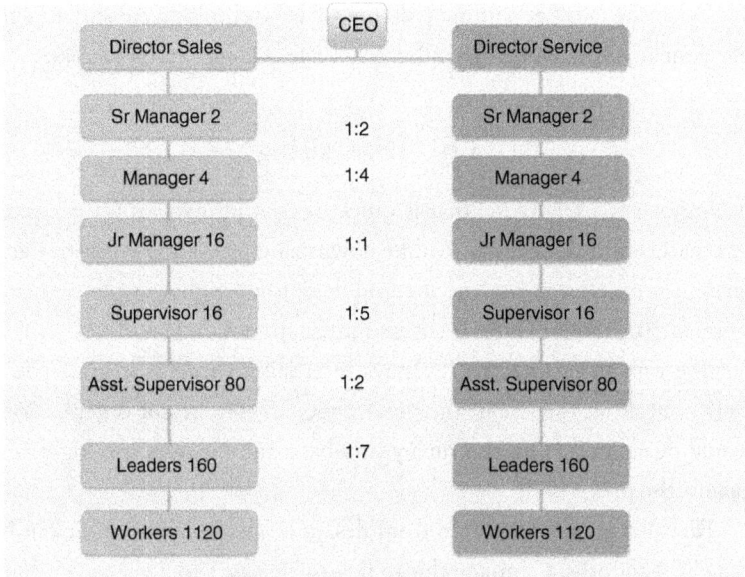

*British Airways delayed and took out of the structure 450 managers—
it was reported that "it had no operational impact on operational
effectiveness". So the question is—what exactly were they all doing—a
very expensive and unneeded overhead.*

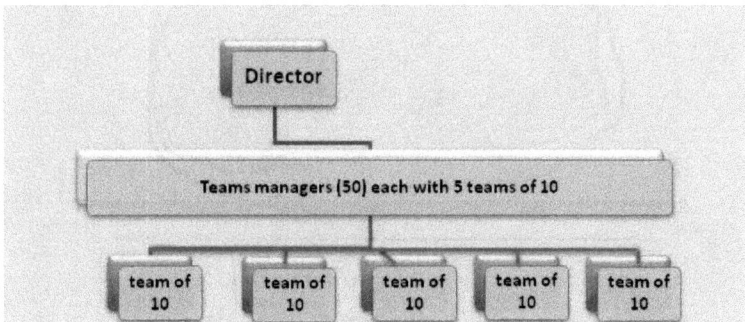

*In the Public sector, Essex County Council removed layers of
management, by twenty percent. Reported on BBC and available on
You Tube, in an interview Essex County Council said "the reduction
of management will have no impact on ECC front line services."*

Downsizing is not without risk, my advice—employ a consultant who has done downsizing before and can provide evidence of its success.

3.6   Rightsizing

Rightsizing is a technique that is quick to do and involves using one of our mathematical formulas. Unlike downsizing, it is almost risk-free and gives very quick returns. The methodology to do rightsizing is by using formula 10. *How to do this* is covered in Chapter 7.

The rightsizing exercise is always interesting to do as it gives you a reality check on the size of the organization. Public sector organizations would be advised to do this on a yearly basis and measure the "rightsize" against the preset budget.

Rightsizing is quick; often from design to implementation, it can be done in 4 months. Compare this to downsizing in 1 to 2 years.

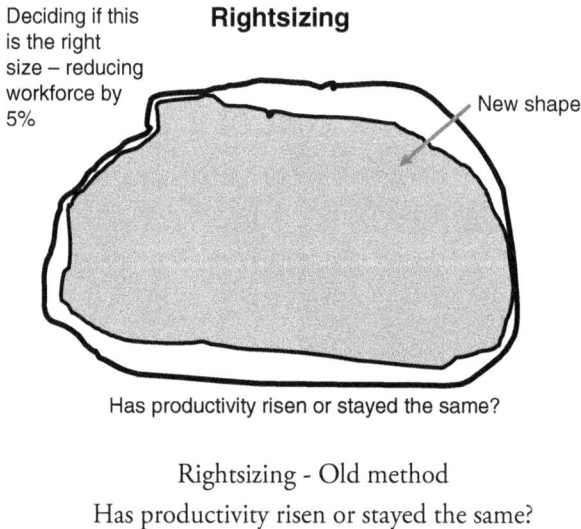

Rightsizing - Old method
Has productivity risen or stayed the same?

CHAPTER 4

Productivity

Sustainable productivity comprises three key components. In New HR Analytics, we must ensure we get this critical data at least annually. The collection of the information is normally linked into the performance appraisal cycle.

The first and perhaps the most obvious of these components is competency. The second area is that of performance, and the final and probably the most neglected is the area of reliability.

Competence + Performance + Reliability = Productivity

4.1   A Word of Caution About the Collection of the Data

Both competence and performance figures normally come from the performance appraisal process. It is very important that you are aware of the statistical significance of collecting this data so that it can be of use to the organization and for your own processing needs. You need to collect all the data so that it's shown on a 1-to-100 scale. In other words, you need exact numbers.

Many organizations use simple tick-box systems which are a poor design—easy for the managers to use but useless for statistical analysis and forecasting.

Unsatisfactory   Below average   Average   Outstanding

In this commonly used method, the manager simply ticks the box where appropriate, either for competence levels or for performance.

The problem then is the range—Unsatisfactory covers a numeric range of 0 to 25, Below average 26 to 50, Average 51 to 75, and Outstanding 76 to 100. For accurate modeling and forecasting, this is just not accurate enough. All of your data collection needs to be on a linear scale 0–100 so that it can be modeled and projected for meaningful and accurate analysis

This is necessary for new workforce planning in all its areas of data collection so that future data manipulation and comparisons can be made.

4.2   Competence

The topic of accurately measuring and valuing competencies has eluded both line manages and HR personnel for years. The numerous books to explain competency frameworks have done nothing but to add complexity and confusion to what is a very simple concept.

4.2.1 What are Competencies and How are they Structured?

The concept of having a competency framework was to enable organizations to benefit from a uniform approach. Competencies are a key observable behavior. There are very important words in that short statement—the first is *key*; when allocating competencies to a job, the focus needs to be on the key competencies. The first and most dramatic mistake organizations make is to allocate as many competencies as possible to cover every single item of work. By so doing, it makes the task of measurement unattainable. Be practical, just focus on what competencies are critical or key to the job, and then the task of measurement and doing training-needs analysis becomes attainable and realistic.

The second important word in the definition of competencies is *behavior*. We can see, measure, and improve behaviors as they consist of skills, knowledge, and experience.

Having a proper competency framework provides organizations with three important outcomes. Competencies provide us with:

- Quality assurance
- Conformance to standards
- Doing things in a safe and legal way.

Without such standards, it is easy to see how mismanagement seeds economic downturns. The current economic downturn is a classic example.

The abuse and misunderstanding of how competencies work has meant that in many organizations their overcomplicated approach has significantly reduced productivity. In an attempt to rectify this, we have set out from scratch how competency frameworks should work as they can be a positive contributor to productivity and more importantly have credibility with the business users. Regardless of what approach you take or which model you use, simplicity and clarity of approach are essential if you are to maximize your investment in your employees.

To get the most from a competency approach, managers need to fully understand how competencies work and why they are important. From practical experience, it comes down to each employee having no more than eight competencies, with six being the average. Key competencies are the ones that really make the difference.

In order to make this clear, there is a complete worked example.

The illustration shows how a Team Leader competency is constructed. The smallest elements are seldom individually rated and training for these parts typically occurs on the job. In Illustration 2, the competency unit is of key interest as this is what we measure and provide training for as the need arises.

The all-important units and their relationship to the competence.

The organizational requirement of competence is important from a training-needs-analysis viewpoint. Although competence affects every individual, the requirement for competence has already been scoped, approved, and funded at the corporate level. Therefore, although competencies appear to be an individual training need, they are really part of the organizational requirement that guarantees and gives conformance to organizational standards.

From a training-needs-analysis point of view, competencies are challenging, especially when the competency does not quite match

The competency framework

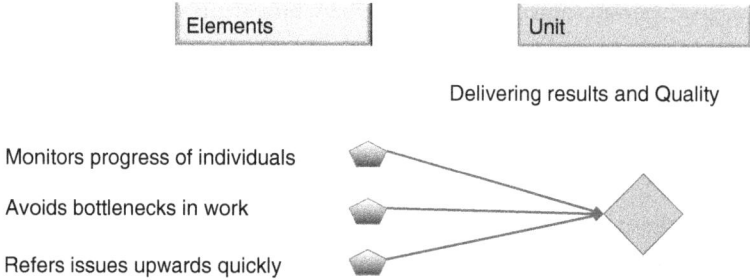

Elements		Unit

Delivering results and Quality

Monitors progress of individuals

Avoids bottlenecks in work

Refers issues upwards quickly

The all important units and their relationship to the competence.

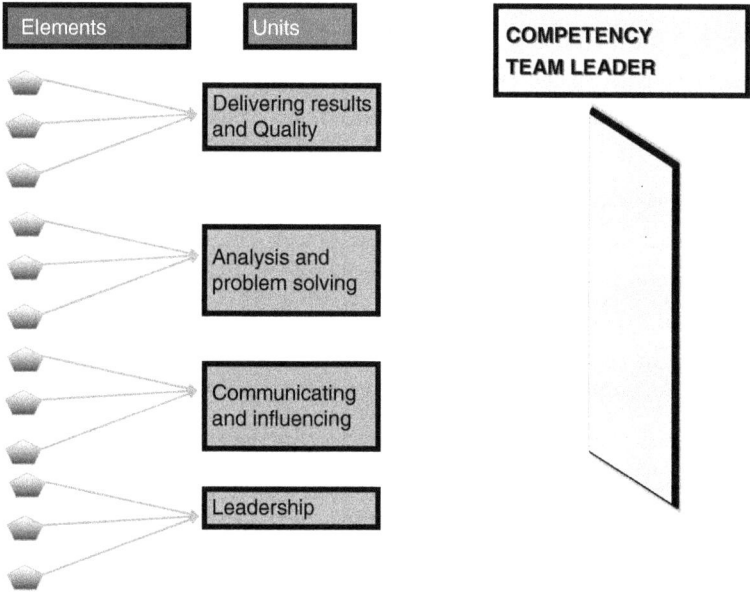

Elements	Units	COMPETENCY TEAM LEADER

Delivering results and Quality

Analysis and problem solving

Communicating and influencing

Leadership

a training course or packaged solution. Identifying the appropriate training to achieve a higher level of competency is subject to broad interpretation.

Before embarking on an exploration of training needs, minimum and maximum standards need to be set for the competency framework within your organization. Although it is unlikely that you know, right off, the minimum, average, and maximum competency levels required in your organization, this data is essential when you conduct your training needs analysis. For example, if the minimum competency level is 50 percent, the average competency is 70 percent and the maximum competency is 85 percent, then you can clearly identify the priority for the training-needs analysis resulting from the competency level of the individual. This is normally recorded at performance appraisal.

Competencies are comprised of three parts: the competency itself, the units that feed into the main competency, and smaller elements that lead to the units which in turn feed into the key competency (see illustrations). This might sound complicated, but in practice the concept is incredibly simple and works well. In performing a training-needs analysis, the most important, efficient part to consider is training at the unit level because that's where training has maximum impact.

Let's look at the example. The competency is team leader. Each page is a unit. You will soon see how this fits in with the previous schema.

TEAM LEADER COMPETENCIES

Competency Unit	Definition	Anchor
Delivering Results and Quality	Directing effort to the achievement of objectives	Ensures satisfactory team delivery of defined goals, overcoming most problems within own area of specialization
Analysis and Problem Solving	Analyzing information effectively and drawing sound conclusions	Evaluates available information, reaching decisions based on key facts and practicality of solutions
Communicating and Influencing	Achieving understanding or gaining acceptance of ideas and proposed action	Prepares case fully, stressing the benefits to be gained and inspiring confidence in own views
Leadership	Getting the best from others	Monitors progress toward achieving clearly defined shared objectives, provides feedback, support, and encouragement to individuals on specific tasks

Unit One—Delivering Results and Quality
   Definition: Directing effort to the achievement of objectives
   Anchor: Ensures satisfactory team delivery of defined goals, overcoming most problems within own area of specialization

Positive Indicators—Elements	Negative Indicators
• Monitors progress of individuals against their targets; encourages achievement • Tackles bottlenecks/backlogs in the system and looks for ways to clear these quickly • Refers issues upwards quickly to get action • Constantly reassesses priorities to focusenergy most productively • Consults external specialists to resolve problems outside own specialist area rapidly • Gets "all hands to the pumps" when dealing with priority, or "emergency" situations • Adopts flexible approach to work; is prepared to commit extra effort whenever necessary • Takes immediate action to rectify slippages	• Does not monitor progress against clear targets • Delays taking decisions until forced to do so • Avoids taking responsibility for own work and that of others • Turns immediately to others for help in resolving situations; does not persist in trying to resolve problems • Fails to respond immediately to slippages within the project

Unit Two—Analysis and Problem Solving

Definition: Analyzing information effectively and drawing sound conclusions

Anchor: Evaluates available information, reaching decisions based on key facts and practical solutions

Positive Indicators—Elements	Negative Indicators
• Utilizes past experience to make standard checks on the reliability of information • Gains as much information as possible from a variety of sources on which to base a decision • Always seeks out facts rather than make assumptions or guess • Considers trade-off of risk vs. gain when coming to conclusions • Bases decisions upon statutory codes of practice where they exist • Bases solutions on the objective facts, not subjective opinion • Considers full implications and benefits of recommendations for the company • Devises objective business case to support	• Takes information at face value; does not cross-check facts • Pays attention only to those facts that suit own position or preferred course of action orinterpretation • Makes decisions based on subjective opinion,or hearsay; doesn't investigate the situations themselves • Values speed of decision making far above careful deliberation even when the time is available

Unit Three—Communicating and Influencing

> Definition: Achieving understanding or gaining acceptance of ideas and proposed action
>
> Anchor: Prepares carefully, stressing the benefits to be gained and inspiring confidence in own views

Positive Indicators—Elements	Negative Indicators
• Prepares facts in advance of meetings • Considers full impact of proposals before putting them forward for consideration • Talks in a positive manner to inspire confidence • Anticipates likely questions and prepares counter-arguments • Keeps the message simple; states the facts and objectives • If unsure of the details, commits to finding out for the next meeting • Answers questions directly • Clarifies the needs of other parties in meetings • Persists in putting forward argument • Uses graphics in presentation where possible • Explains logic behind changes	• Delivers an unstructured argument • Makes up arguments when own case is questioned • Presents in a flat and monotone fashion • Gives way quickly when others raise counter-arguments • Loses interest if agreement isn't forthcoming • Uses jargon or technical terms others may not understand • Loses patience with those who do not appear to understand the argument put forward

Unit Four—Leadership

> Definition: Getting the best from others
>
> Anchor: Monitors team morale, provides feedback, support, and encouragement to individuals on achieving objectives

Positive Indicators—Elements	Negative Indicators
• Sets realistic but challenging goals by • breaking down overall targets/objectives • Makes time available to staff to share expertise/knowledge • Conducts regular meetings to review individuals' performance • Conducts quarterly appraisal meetings that focus on development and potential for progression against objectives • Gives negative feedback in private; points out implications of approach taken • Conducts regular team meetings to communicate information/review team progress and team goals and to praise successes and build team spirit	• Maintains distance from staff • Works on an "us" and "them" basis • Is destructive when giving staff negative feedback; uses authoritarian approach, is sarcastic or punitive in making comments • Does not communicate successes to the team • Does not make time available to staff • Fails to praise work well done; takes good performance of staff for granted

Positive Indicators—Elements	Negative Indicators
• Identifies training needs of staff and supports with training opportunities • Regulates workload of staff; doesn't over-burden them • Gives staff clear instructions as to what is required on tasks, and to what standard • Ensures team members are fully briefed on task plans and the background • Provides constructive feedback to help individuals overcome problems or improve their performance • Understands what motivates individual members of staff, e.g., pay, career progression • Makes it clear to staff which types of decisions they should/should not make	• Expects others to be motivated as a matter of course; does not make active attempts to motivate the team • Adopts a controlling approach; does not encourage staff to take ownership of their work • Offers no support for personal development

4.2.2 Measuring Competency Levels and Getting the Best from Training

What's the competitive advantage of this approach, e.g., focusing on measuring only units? First, we need to be realistic about setting organizational competency standards in line with the KEY competencies. In the illustration, the minimum competency standard is set at 50 percent.

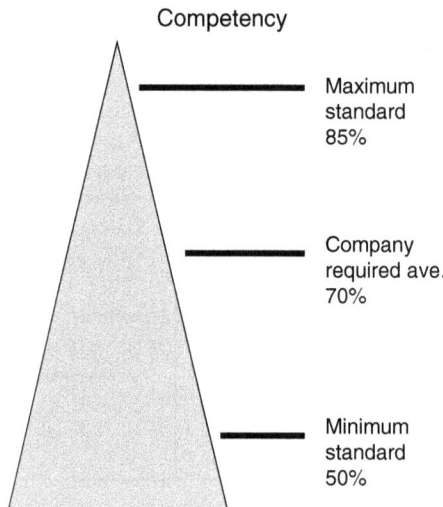

Competency

Maximum standard 85%

Company required ave. 70%

Minimum standard 50%

4.3   Performance

4.3.1 Introduction to Performance

Performance is raw output, essentially how much we do. Performance is measured in a number of ways including:

- Speed
- Time
- Efficiency
- Unit cost
- Volume

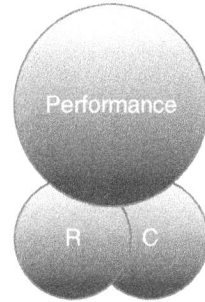

Most companies are overstaffed by 15 to 20 percent and of course much higher in the Public Sector. Published figures by the Government in the UK showed that there were 50 percent too many people in the Public Sector and specifically in the Public Health Service. It was reported by McKenzie consulting that 1 in 10 employees in the Health Service could be dispensed with. In a survey of Public Sector employees, 89 percent felt that budgets and public spending were managed inefficiently.

What performance is expected should be very clear in the contract of employment, although companies should seek legal counsel in this regard as employment law statutes vary geographically on this issue. On the other hand, performance levels above those required should be locked into a bonus or reward system. If the original criteria are correctly set, it should be difficult for employees to do more in the same time, since in theory they are working at their optimal level. So you will need to make the decision—bonus or overtime—but not both.

Performance expectations (above required performance) should be established during the performance appraisal and updated throughout the year.

Measuring of performance can be done in three different ways, and these are approached depending on the type of business you work in, the country you are employed in, and finally the culture of the company or organization that you are part of.

1. *Performance measure by time worked.* This works well if you have managers who really do manage. Also, certain cultures are very

work-focused and when they are at work, work really hard. This particularly applies to China where hard work by the hour is part of the culture. In 2014/15, a survey was carried out in the Middle East to determine how many hours people worked in a 40-hour week:

Talented workers—17 percent worked 32 hours a week

Average workers—61 percent worked 22 hours a week

Poor performers—22 percent worked 5 hours a week

  I have displayed this data in many (non-Asian) countries and very few people seem surprised about the results; particularly those in the public sector.

2. *Performance through individual target setting.* This is a real winner but it carries with it a big warning. Properly set and monitored targets with big bonuses produce massive results, provided

  a. that at the end of the year the bonus is not subjected to forced ranking

  b. that the bonus must be subjected to the average competence and reliability scores being achieved

  c. that the bonus is directly aligned with organizational achievement

3. *Performance through team target setting.* Very much the same criteria as the above, but using a Hopper Bonus scheme where all participants (The Team) need to meet the score requirement for competence and reliability before any bonus can be earned.

Companies that take their eyes off this soon find themselves in real financial difficulty.

There are three approaches to get performance, and each has its own advantages and disadvantages.

Self-motivated staff—these employees are painstakingly recruited and just know what needs to be done. They require little motivation or supervision, and work whatever hours are needed. They are normally bonused via some form of share/stock option scheme.

The second is the managed workforce—employed but not trusted. Management runs a strict and inflexible routine. In this instance, performance is achieved by hours worked, the manager taking responsibility for prescribing work and making sure it is done in the time allocated.

The third and most abused is the setting of objectives and stretch targets. The old-style managers are just not good at doing this and are constantly undermined by having forced ranked bonus schemes determining who gets what bonus at the end of the year.

4.3.2 Consistent Theme in Performance—It Must Be Measured

Regardless of which of the three schemes you use, the approach for measurement is the same as for competency. Management needs to set minimum company standards, and top-end figures for performance.

As with competency (quality), no bonus or additional payments should be made for anything below required average standard. In fact, if required performance is not achieved then employees' basic salaries ought to be reduced. Check this out carefully as it may not be legally possible although I think it's morally right. All of this highlights the need for thorough recruitment practices; just look at how good Google are at this—and look at their bottom-line performance figures.

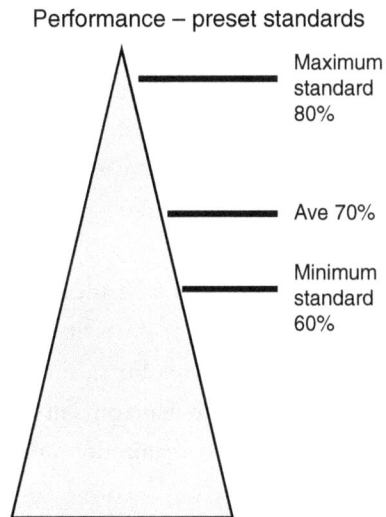

Performance – preset standards

Maximum standard 80%

Ave 70%

Minimum standard 60%

You may be wondering why productivity is not at 100 percent on our chart. Well, there are two very separate components that affect this. The first is TIME. In a 38-hour week—no one can work 38 hours, we have PT&C time plus a lunch break. So at best, the working week will only be 30 hours of available time.

Poor overall performance is then compensated for (by the managers) who demand more staff—resulting in overstaffed organizations.

4.4   Reliability

Reliability is a dimension of value that is very rarely measured by workforce management. So what is reliability and why should we take it seriously? We already know the costs of an employee and what that cost is per day (explained in Chapter 7). We also know the cost of an employee per hour. Reliability is a measurement of whether or not that person works for the hours that they are paid.

Unreliable people tend to commence work late, often leave early, and have a remarkably high level of unsubstantiated sick leave.

The two key areas for us to focus on are sickness and unsubstantiated days off (either from uncertified sickness or other reasons). Although this sounds more like absenteeism, for our purpose, we call it reliability.

Other areas of unreliability are also important, but the main ones are those highlighted.

Why we need to get on top of this is because it cost lots of money directly and has a negative effect on employee morale indirectly. That is why measuring reliability is increasingly an important factor in workforce management and reporting the cost of unreliable people is a major business cost factor.

Fortunately, mathematically it is now possible to calculate by individual, section, or department the direct cost of reliability. We have developed a formula for this; this can also be projected using our predictive workforce management tools showing the cost over 5, 10, and 15 years. For all organizations, this figure is so significant that it cannot be ignored.

If we look at an example of one person coming to work late every day (just 30 minutes), they have 14 uncertified sick days in the year, then what is the cost in reliability for that employee for 1 year:

$$£46 \times .5 \times 226 = £5198$$
$$£46 \times 8 \times 14 = £5152$$
$$\text{Total cost} = £10{,}350$$

If 20 percent of our 3,000-strong workforce fall into this category, then the real cost per year is $600 \times £10{,}350 = £6{,}210{,}000$. DO I HAVE YOUR ATTENTION NOW?

So for our three time scales of 5, 10, and 15 years, that's:

$$5 \times £6210000 = £31{,}050{,}000$$
$$10 \times £6210000 = £62{,}100{,}000$$
$$15 \times £6210000 = £93{,}150{,}000$$

From work on reliability carried out over a number of years, these are very conservative figures. If this does not grab your attention—then do the calculation based on Birmingham City Council's figures:

17.9 days off each year for each or the 50,000 people.

100	=	0
75	=	96.5
50	=	193
25	=	289.5
0	=	386

When gathering data, we use formula 2 and then the figures are converted into a linear scale so that we can correlate them for other comparative work if needed.

Using your facts, you can now do a benchmark to find out how reliable your employees are and what's the cost to the organization. It's management's job to rectify the fault if you have a big issue here—not yours. You have identified the problem—costed it and provided the management information on the cost to the organization. Ongoing monitoring will make this a key Human Capital measurement factor.

It would be prudent to come up with a figure of where you expect the organization to be on the chart—100 percent is not realistic.

Thus in 2012, using an existing formula (the Bradford formula), we have mathematically adjusted the output so that the output scale runs on a 0-to-100 scale with the indicators showing when counseling is needed, when a first verbal warning is given, when the first written warning is given, when a written warning is given, and when a final written warning and dismissal is given.

Using a new piece of software it's now an integrated package, which can be used, with competence measurement and productivity measurement.

The data are fed into this program and the appropriate actions to be taken are displayed to the manager so that there can be no oversight, slippage, or ability to "forget" to take action.

As I mentioned before, reliability is one of three key indicators, which together equal productivity. It is important that any decisions on increments, bonus, allowances, or promotion are only taken viewing the total picture. Very often, reliability is not taken into account during interviews or for selection and promotion. Poor reliability has a marked effect on other employees' motivation. To such an extent this has a serious impact on organizational efficiency, if it is left unchecked.

Financially the cost of poor reliability is enormous. Not only in straight financial terms (e.g., the person's salary), but in terms of missed deadlines, slippages, and lower quality standards. Therefore, I'm sure you can see that reliability is a key indicator and essential for our dashboard.

4.4.1 Can Poor Reliability be Identified?

Significant evidence exists that likely poor reliability can be shown using personality profilers.

Other research has been carried out looking at the impact of job satisfaction and absenteeism and this seems to be clear evidence of positive correlations between high-frequency absenteeism (many short absences from work) and dissatisfaction in the job.

This further shows the importance of doing regular staff satisfaction surveys to insure and measure the relationship between absenteeism and the staff satisfaction scale. This is so important that it features on our dashboard productivity indicator scale.

4.4.2 Projections of Lost Time Through Poor Reliability

Using formula 2 and the appropriate software, it is possible to get a linear numeric score (0 to 100) that shows reliability. By then modeling the data

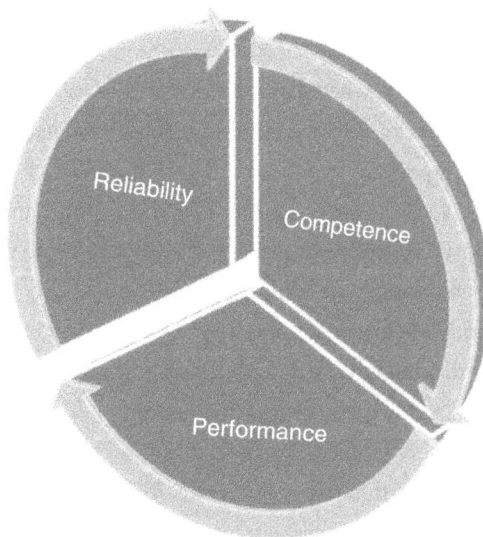

using a Monte Carlo–type simulator, you can project the reliability factor for 5 to 10 years in the future and then establish what the financial costs will be to the organization.

4.4.3 Reliability and Recruitment

Reliability is very important when recruiting. Reliability—if an important part of the job should be identified on a Personality Profiler. High Conscientiousness scores are good predictors of reliability. Failure to find this out on recruitment can have serious consequences for the very best of workforce plans. This was revealed when G4S, a security company, had

> Just four of the 58 staff expected to report for duty at the Hilton Hotel in Gateshead, Tyne and Wear, showed up, one of whom later disappeared.

been awarded the security contract for the Olympic games—hosted in the UK. The recruitment process was flawed and the complete lack of testing for reliability produced headline news in most of the UK newspapers as staff failed to turn up for work.

The following information was printed by the Daily Mail newspaper:

4.5   Use of the Three Pieces of Data

Using the software, the three data streams from competence, performance, and reliability are modeled to show if the person has achieved the minimum requirement—if so then is the appropriate trigger for entering a bonus scheme, being eligible for an increment or for being considered for development. Low figures can be modeled to show the cost of below-average performance and appropriate action taken.

4.6   Training's Role in Performance Improvement

Training has a very important role in improving competence and performance. Over 95 percent of all training carried out is competence based. That is good if compliance is your major objective, but training is missing a trick in not doing more to improve performance. This is due to a deep-rooted belief that competent staff will automatically result in high-performing staff—this of course is untrue. In the following case study, training had spent a lot of time and effort in training sales staff on the ergonomics and safety relating to using their workstations, correct posture, distance from the screen, and so on. As you will see from the case study what a huge difference training can make if properly focused on performance.

4.7   Performance - Typing Case Study

Background

This is a call center employing 200 sales people, and the main part of their work when talking to the customers on the phone is to enter the information direct into the sales computer system.

When interviewed, their skills as telephone sales people are assessed. It has recently come to light that they were not asked about their keyboarding skills. When reassuring their skill for keyboarding speed (the system does this), it has transpired that the average speed is 14 words per minute.

The sales manager has put in a request to employ an additional 15 people due to increased business.

The training function has been asked if they can improve productivity—if so by how much and what is the likely value if this is done.

Fixed Data

Cost of the training equipment and typing software: **£35,000**
Time to do the training: **3 days**
ESUC: **£46.00 per hour**
PWD: **226**
Training cost per person per day: £125.78
Training's TASK
1. Establish the actual cost of the training
2. Establish the cost (value) of one typed word

3. How many extra words would be needed to break even
4. What is a reasonable improvement that this typing training can achieve—words in excess of 18wpm
5. What is the added value and how does that compare to the employment of the proposed extra 15 people.

Calculations

What is the total cost of the training
Cost of equipment and software = £35,000
Training costs £125.78 (IHIHT) × 3days × 200people = £75,468
ESUC cost 200 people × 24hours × £46per hour = £220,800
Total expenditure £110,688

Establish the cost of one word
Divide £46 by 60 =.76
Divide that figure by 18wpm =.042
Cost of one word per person =**.042**
Latest Techniques in Workforce Planning 2015   52
How many extra words are needed to cover the cost
Divide £35,000 by the yearly cost of one word for the entire group
Value of word pm .042 × 60mins (to give you hours × by 8 hours)
    (1 day = **£20.44**)
Daily value £20.44 × 200 number of people × 226PWD (see page 69) (days in the year) = value of one word for the group in 1 year
    £923,888
Divide into total training costs = words needed in excess of 18wpm to cover the costs **ONE WORD! (can't do less than one)**

Conclusion

After the training, the actual performance increase was an improvement giving 30wpm.

In doing the final financial calculation, it was agreed that nobody typed for a solid 8 hours a day and it was agreed correctly that the figure be reduced to 6 hours.

The financial result was that none of the proposed 15 staff were employed as all the capacity needed had been provided by just one piece of training.

The real value of performance-based training is a vital aid to business efficiency. Some performance-based training activities are as follows:

- Commitment budgeting to deliver agreed budgets within or under budget
- Managing projects to deliver ahead of target and within budget
- Predictive workforce planning
- Re-negotiating existing contracts
- Train the trainer—to achieve more training in-house
- NLP for sales staff
- Converting cost centers to profit centers
- Setting and managing performance targets
- Innovation thinking to reduce operating cost

Software

New workforce planning requires very specific software. This is not expensive, most being $100, but is essential for doing many of the calculations in this book and also for rightsizing. All of the software we use are supplied and supported by Duncan Williamson, e-mail: duncanwil@gmail.com

Films

There are two supporting films you may be interested in; both filmed in 2016. The first is about how you collect workforce planning data using performance appraisal. The second explains in detail how the MILLER model works for predicting organizational change.

CHAPTER 5

Trends and Correlations

5.1   Trends

Trends give us time to plan and time to advise and alert other areas of the business. Failure to do this by workforce planners often has serious consequences in terms of panic recruitment and instability through competency drop. In this chapter, we will look at some of the formulas that work and give examples of how they may be used, using some current case studies. Beware in the area of trend analysis, as these are most of the old academic formulas that either don't work well in practice or which have been replaced with relevant software.

Some of the trends you would constantly review are:

- Age
- Sickness
- Competence (see chapter on Efficiency Dashboard)
- Performance (see chapter on Efficiency Dashboard)
- Reliability (see chapter on Efficiency Dashboard)
- Predictable turnover
- Turnover
- Staff satisfaction
- Productivity
- Workforce requirement

All of the time, trends can be plotted using Excel. Excel is also a great base for using other software such as simulators—Monte Carlo–types for predictive forecasting and where comparable trends are compared using a correlation formula and other associated workforce planning software.

5.2   Turnover Trends

5.2.1 Introduction

It is very important to get to grips with why we use turnover trends and what management information we are to deliver. It may be of use to know how many people leave the organization in a year—what's more important is to be able to spot trends and act on them to ensure that the organization has the right amount of human resource at any given time and in every circumstance.

a) As far as turnover (often referred to as wastage) is concerned, we have two completely different factors. Predictable turnover, for example, when people will retire or where we have people on long-term sickness and we will retire them. This information is known and predictable.

b) What is of greater interest is the stability of the organization and the effect on the organization of random turnover, that is, people leaving for whatever reason. It is this information that provides us with critical management information. Using predictive techniques, we can then forecast likely trends in our organization.

Using both sets of information, we can then fairly accurately know in each future year, how many people we will need to recruit, in what department, and what skills specialty is needed.

5.2.2 The Labor Turnover Index

This index is basically the number of leavers expressed as a percentage of average employees. It is also known as the "crude" turnover (or wastage) index. However, in certain circumstances, it can be quite a meaningless statistic and very misleading if given to managers to make decisions.

The simplest measure involves calculating the number of leavers in a period (usually a year) as a percentage of the number employed during the same period. This is known as the "crude wastage rate" and is calculated as follows:

Number of leavers, divided by average number employed × 100

For example, if a business has 150 leavers during the year and, on average, it employed 2,000 people during the year, the labor turnover figure would be 7.5 percent.

$$\frac{150 \times 100}{2,000} = LTI7.5\%$$

The importance of this to workforce planning is that what is needed is a measure which can predict future wastage and take into account both staying and leaving characteristics.

In an effort to provide a prediction of wastage for use with manpower planning, the labor turnover index, being so unstable and reflecting changes in length of service, may be little short of useless.

Also, statistically, it's not a good idea to include any employees who have been with the company for less than a year. This first year reflects poor recruitment, where employees don't like the job or where the employee finds the job not living up to their expectations and leaves. Also, this first year period also includes the probationary period—where low scoring on competence, productivity, or reliability results in dismissal.

Although the labor turnover index (LTI) has been criticized quite heavily, in its defense it is easy to compute, and given a stable labor force, (may) be useful—advice here—forget it.

5.3   The Modified Labor Stability Index (Formula 2)

What is the purpose of this formula? This information is vital to management (not managers) on the stability of the organization's Human Capital. Here, we are looking for potential trends, which may affect the business stability.

To overcome the problems with the LTI, the Labor Stability Index (LSI) was designed. This gives you a much better idea of what's going on in real business terms, particularly in turbulent times.

When using this index, remove all of the employees that have less than 1 year's service to give a statistically more reliable picture. Also, all predictable leavers should be removed (people who in that period will retire and long-term sickness leavers in the same yearly period).

The calculation is then done using formula 2.

$$\frac{\text{Total employed with more than 1 year's service now} - (\text{retirees \& long-term sickness}) \text{ in this period} \times 100}{\text{Total employed 1 year ago} - (\text{retirees and long-term sickness leavers}) \text{ in this period}} = \textbf{LSI}$$

$$\frac{3{,}000 - (30 + 6) \times 100}{3{,}200 - (20 + 10)} = \text{LSI } 93.50\%$$

5.4   Cohort Analysis Formula 4

Cohort analysis requires following the "rate of survival" of a group (cohort) of employees through time. An example would be a large graduate recruitment program.

The following example shows the cohort analysis and from that you can plot the resulting survival curve which shows the percentage of employees surviving (and remaining) at different points in time.

In statistical practice, this is answered by a goodness-of-fit test which is concerned with whether the observed deviations from the fitted curve are such as could be accounted for by chance. In our view, this is not usually the question of practical importance.

We really need to know whether the use of the fitted distribution will be sufficiently accurate for practical purposes and this can only be decided in the context of the problem in hand. It can well happen, for example, that a fit which would be rejected by a formal test of significance leads to predictions of sufficient accuracy for a particular purpose.

However, we regard this not as an argument for disregarding goodness-of-fit altogether but for interpreting the results sensibly, with due regard for the uses to which the analysis is to be put.

If a graphical method has been used, a good deal can be learnt from an inspection of the plot.

If the points show a marked departure from linearity as in the exponential fit, one would clearly be very wary of using the fitted distribution for any purpose which depended on extrapolating the line.

If, on the other hand, the points were linear but subject to a wide scatter about the line, we would suspect that the form of the distribution fitted was satisfactory but that its parameters could not be determined very precisely.

The extent of the scatter would also give us some indication of the error of estimates of the survivor function made by reading off values from the line.

5.4.1 Predicting Turnover (Wastage)

The easy way is to use the modified LSI formula, which will have excluded natural wastage (retirements) and long-term sickness. Both of which are predictable. It then uses current turnover (wastage) data and simply uses a Monte Carlo–type simulator to project the predictable turnover for the next 3 years realistically which is about as far ahead as is safe.

5.5   Use of Correlations

The correlation or comparing of similar types of data allows us predictively to see what evidence exists to make future decisions. For example, in industry X, do employees who receive a lot of training outperform those who have little or no training?

Doing a correlation would give us the answer and at the same time would enable us to make a sound decision on either, more or less investment in training, depending on the result.

Using the evidence of correlations stops us from making judgments on what we feel or is a good idea and allows us to act professionally based on the facts.

The list is endless; your role will be to decide what is of value to your organization and is relevant.

Some examples:

Smokers—sickness

Performance appraisal scores—productivity on the job

Performance—age

Age group—sickness

Competence—personality type

Productivity—sex

Competence—personality type

Duration with the company–reliability

Time with company—promotion level

There are three principal correlation formulas.

- Pearson's Moment Correlation formula
- Spearman's Correlation formula
- Kendall's W formula.

In workforce planning, we tend to use Pearson's formula 99.9 percent of the time. The formula can be worked out long hand—but I can't imagine why you would want to do this except that you can show off your prowess in mathematics. There are many software packages available such as analyze it www.analyse-it.com/products/standard/correlation.aspx.

These correlation packages sit in Microsoft Excel and simple take the data and import it into the package and produce the r score.

The correlation or fit of the data is shown as its closeness to 1. So scores from .65 up to 1 would show the strength of the correlation. Below .65 there is no relationship worth considering. Correlations can be either positive or negative; the strength is still of importance.

Looking at the formula, we can have a go at working out an example from data gathered from a consultancy project in Western America.

Pearson's moment correlation Formula 1

$$ r = \frac{\sum XY - \frac{(\sum X) * (\sum Y)}{N}}{\sqrt{\left(\sum X^2 - \frac{(\sum X)^2}{N} \right) * \left(\sum Y^2 - \frac{(\sum Y)^2}{N} \right)}} $$

The issue we have been asked to solve is when new employees are tested they are given both Maths and Science test papers, the company concerned wants to know—is there a relationship between these tests. If so, can one of the tests be dropped, this would save an estimated $750,000 p.a.

The sample size was over 1,500—in this example, it has been reduced purely to give you an example and encourage you to have a go.

N = the number in the sample

X = The Maths score (range 0 to 20)

Y = The Science score (range 0 to 20)

Example 1: Data

Student:	Math (X):	Science (Y):	X2	Y2	X*Y
A	11	11	$11^2 =$	$11^2 =$	=
B	13	10	$13^2 =$	$10^2 =$	=
C	18	17	$18^2 =$	$17^2 =$	=
D	12	13	$12^2 =$	$13^2 =$	=
E	16	14	$16^2 =$	$14^2 =$	=
N =	$\Sigma X =$	$\Sigma Y =$	$\Sigma X^2 =$	$\Sigma Y^2 =$	$\Sigma XY =$

Have a go and see if you can do it!

Example 1: Equation

$$r = \frac{\sum XY - \dfrac{\left(\sum X\right) * \left(\sum Y\right)}{N}}{\sqrt{\left(\sum X^2 - \dfrac{\left(\sum X\right)^2}{N}\right) * \left(\sum Y^2 - \dfrac{\left(\sum Y\right)^2}{N}\right)}}$$

Put in the numbers.

Step three—Finish the calculation

ANSWER: r =

In other words, there is a strong positive correlation between marks in maths and science. So what's the added value comment?

In this instance, there is no need to do both tests—thus saving $750,000 p.a.

Answers available in Appendix 1

The opportunities for exploring correlations in the organization are endless; so please remember that our job in doing this is to provide the organization with useful information, with a solution or recommendation that will add significant value.

Technical information if you need it—The "coefficient of determination", r^2:

You can get a good idea of how good a correlation really is, by squaring the correlation coefficient. r^2 is called the "coefficient of determination", and it tells you how much the variance in one of the variables can be accounted for by a knowledge of the other.

Suppose, for example, that there was a .5 correlation between I.Q. score and subsequent academic performance $.50^2 = .25$. This means that only 25 percent of the variation in academic performance can be accounted for in terms of its relationship with I.Q.; 75 percent of the variation in academic performance must therefore be attributable to factors other than I.Q. We would therefore be rash to assign children to different schools, etc. purely on the basis of I.Q. score.

Note that calculating the coefficient of determination (r^2) emphasizes the fact that the scale on which Pearson's r is ranged (i.e., -1 to $+1$) is not a linear scale: a correlation of .8 is not twice as good as one of .4, it is *much* better!

A .8 correlation between two variables means that knowledge of one variable accounts for 64 percent of the variance in the other

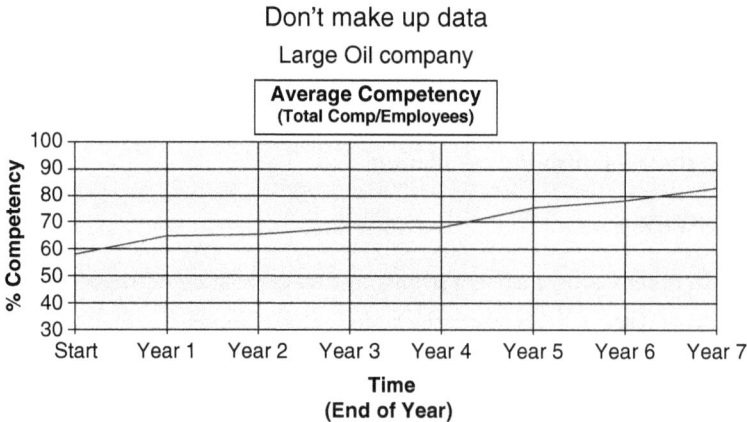

Don't make up data

Large Oil company

Average Competency
(Total Comp/Employees)

(.82 =.64 = 64%). In contrast, a.4 correlation accounts for only 16 percent of the variance, and a .2 correlation accounts for only 4 percent of the variance! In short, the closer a correlation is to −1 to +1, then the stronger it is, and this process accelerates as one nears −1 or +1.

It's sobering to think that many correlations in psychological research are around the .3 to .5 mark. This means that although they may be "real" correlations, they are virtually useless in practical terms (i.e., as a means of making predictions, given knowledge of one of the variables concerned).

This chart was presented to the senior management team showing the progress that fresh graduates will make in the company. When challenged on the figures, the gentleman concerned admitted, "I made them up" but was convinced, based on no empirical data that this was going to happen!

CHAPTER 6

Use of Predictive Techniques

6.1 Concepts of Forecasting

The old Manpower planning functions were masters at telling managers what they already were aware of—in other words, they were flooded with retrospective information. This data unprocessed, has very little if any use at all, but consumes management time in trying to understand it. We now have very good predictive software and it's this significant difference that will help us to transform retrospective data to meaningful and valuable information which will aid efficiency, give competitive edge, and also improve organizational efficiency.

Good news for workforce planners—you will (somewhere) have most of the data you need to do predictive forecasting. The bad news, some of it may not be statistically sound. For use either in correlations or in predictive techniques, collected data need to be provided on a 1-to-100 scale. Many so-called performance appraisal systems have a four-box category for marking, given titles such as Unsatisfactory, Satisfactory, Good, and Outstanding. Data collected in this way are statistically dead in the water. As each category has a range of 0 to 25, it is far too wide to be of any real use. A cheap but effective solution— if the appraisal is a paper-based system, the need is to simply draw a line under the four boxes and make that a 1-to-100 scale and get the managers to simply indicate on the line the appropriate score.

From Chapter 4, you will recall that we are collecting productivity information from three prime sources:

- Competency
- Performance
- Reliability

Each of these scores will appear for each individual so that we can do predictions, by individual, by department, or for the organization.

6.1.1 Software to Use

The internationally accepted software to be used is a Monte Carlo simulator. This makes the whole job quick and easy. Various packages exist, all of which do the same job, but they vary in price from $100to $5,000 plus.

6.1.1.1 Example 1

When doing predictive calculations, it is important to remember that the information must add value to the organization and have with it a recommendation or advice.

In this example, we are looking at an organization that employs 13,000 people. We are specifically interested in the competency levels.

Year	Competency (organizational) as a percentage
1995	70
1996	65
1997	68
1998	60
1999	64
2000	71
2001	72
2002	61
2003	64
2004	68
2005	61
2006	69
2007	67
2008	69
2009	67
2010	62
2011	67
2012	67

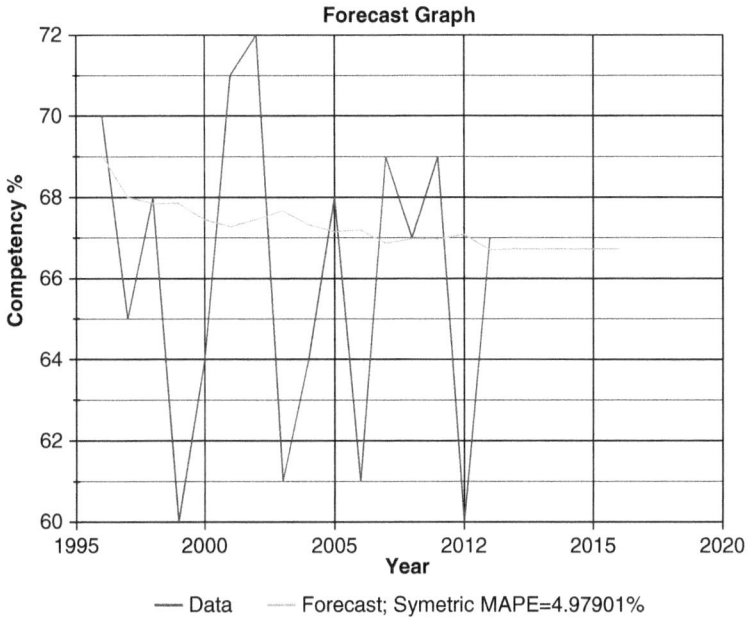

Forecast Graph

— Data   — Forecast; Symetric MAPE=4.97901%

The data used have come from performance appraisal scores and have been stored in an Excel spreadsheet by departments. We know from the presets shown in Chapter 4 that the required average is 75 percent. In this example, the data had been reported, but it was buried in a mass of other statistics every year, but nothing had been done about it.

Once you can see the prediction, you can recognize the problem. The competency level is nowhere near the required 70 percent. Further examination of other related data showed that there was less investment in training during this period and an increase in the accident rate within the company, and that the turnover had also steadily increased.

Recommendation: if the 70 percent is still to be the company average competency level, then an increase in the level of competency-based training is needed; the cost of which would be justified by a lower turnover rate of 3 percent and reduced accident rate.

6.1.1.2 Example: Sysco

Sysco, like many other companies in the world, was looking to improve efficiency. They undertook a study to determine what impact the cost of turnover was having on their business. At the time of the survey and projection, their turnover rate was about average, but increasing, particularly in their lorry delivery area. The extract below is from an interview with Ken Carring; once he had identified the problem and then taken action—the benefits speak for themselves.

Ken Carring: Senior Vice President and Chief Administrative Officer: "75% of SYSCO's costs are people-related expenses and for us what that means is about three billion dollars of expenses and so when we can move retention of our marketing associates, of which we have about ten thousand marketing associates, if we can move that retention rate from 70% to 80%, for us, that means approximately, with ten thousand marketing associates, that's approximately $50 thousand per marketing associate, turns out to be over $70 million of savings per year.

we've moved our marketing associate retention from 70% to 82%. Our delivery associates, which are a very critical success to SYSCO because they know the customers, they're the ones that the customers rely on getting their groceries to them on time and in the condition that they expected and in order to get them on time you need to have the same person going to the same customer on a regular basis.

For us, we were able to move our delivery associates from about 65% retention rate to 85% and we've costed out the training and hiring loss for delivery associates to be about $35 thousand, so again, almost another $50 million in savings when we made that kind of contribution, which for SYSCO investors that's about every 5 million, is a penny per share, so there's 10 cents right there."

6.1.1.3 Example: BMW 2015

BMW did a number of projections relating to the age of its workforce. It showed that it had an ageing workforce (unusual for the automotive industry). Productivity increases were planned and the challenge was how to make an ageing workforce more productive.

Rather than think of removing or replacing its ageing workforce, BMW asked a simple but very effective question to its older workers:

What do you need to help you work better?

What happened?

- The decision was made to help the older people to work better by changing their working environment.
- How much did this cost?
  - Wooden flooring   €5,000.00
  - Barbershop type chairs   €1,000.00
  - Orthopaedic footwear   €2,000.00
  - Angled monitors with large print   No cost
  - Magnifying lenses   €1,000.00
  - Adjustable work tables   No cost
  - Large handled gripping tools   No cost—How?
  - Stackable transport containers   No cost
  - Manual hoisting cranes   €1,000.00
  - Management time to run project   €10,000.00
  - **Total cost**   plus salary   €50,000.

The result

In the area where this was done, productivity went up by 7 percent and sickness dropped to below the factory average.
Clearly not all of the benefits could be attributed to workforce planning, but in all three examples it shows the power of predictive techniques.

6.2   Predictive Forecasting for Growth

One of the traditional formulas still used by workforce planners for predictive forecasting does not work in practice. The half life cycle formula has been replaced by predictive software and a better understanding of key indicators. It's important for all predictive forecasting to understand how the business works and what the link is between work done and support needed. These ratios must be worked out in a sound and methodical way, as the data become the foundation for accurate forecasting.

A) First, establish the right size of the organization using formula 10. You might not use this information straightaway; you do need to factor it in for long-term forecasting.

B) Next, establish key workload figures. This does not only apply to the private sector, but to any organization. First, find out what the key production people produce each day. A good example of this is in the case study in Chapter 9, Lane Engineering. Here, we have established that production workers produce 17 units per person per day and packing works each pack 25.5 units per person each day.

C) Once workloads have been established, it is very straightforward to calculate how many support staff are needed to make the organization work effectively.

Now that you have the information, it's very straightforward to be able to do a predictive chart that will show how many people are needed to support any future growth plans. The added value is that you will be able to get the gearing ratios spot on.

N.B. With expansion and contraction, you have to factor in the three types of employees—this factor must also be used when forecasting from predictable wastage.

You need to know what category of employee is leaving or is being replaced. E.g., If (based on the 2010 survey) you had 10 poor performers leaving—it is likely that their work could be done by just three average performers. It is vital that you know the percentages of poor performers, average performers, and high performers when doing any of the expansion or contraction calculations. This must be worked out for your own organization so that all your workforce forecasting can be accurate.

In the past, many forecasting mistakes have been made based on the assumption that employees all work the hours they are paid for—this is simply not true and we need to take a very pragmatic view on this.

The survey which was completed late in 2014/15 showed that:

Poor performers worked for 5 hours a week and accounted for 17 percent of the workforce.

Average performers worked for 22 hours a week and accounted for 61 percent of the workforce.

High performers worked for 32 hours a week and accounted for 22 percent of the workforce.

The survey was carried out in the Middle East, specifically large companies, 110 in total, and focused on real work hours.

6.3   Predictive Forecasting for Contraction

The biggest fault I have seen in contraction circumstances—particularly in the world financial crisis in 2012 is the delay and reluctance to take action. This has been the downfall of many large and successful organizations. We witnessed Kodak, a world brand name file for bankruptcy protection and Nokia stock referred to as "junk status" in the financial press.

It has also been apparent that the old style manpower planning departments seem to have been caught on their back foot focusing on the wrong or inappropriate data.

Actions that need to be taken are very similar for growth with the exception of the positioning of formula 10. Formula 10 is the trigger and the absolute minimum number to work with. From experience, most organizations we have worked with have reduced by 20 percent without an undue strain on the organization.

Using Lane Engineering as an example, it's very obvious that a massive saving in staff numbers lies not with the workers but in the areas of management and auxiliary support. As with growth, it's easy to sort out the right numbers for any reduction in production brought about by declining market demand.

6.3.1   A Word of Caution

There are two factors that workforce planners need always to keep their eye on.

1. **Predictable turnover or wastage, this includes:**
   Retirements
   Long-term sickness Predictable turnover
2. **Unpredictable turnover**
   Death in service
   Defection of staff to competitors
   Immigration
   Non-returners to work (mothers not returning after starting a family)
   Taking early retirement

Every organization will have its own additions to the above lists; so don't take the above as absolutes.

6.4   Planning for Succession

First—it is unreasonable and totally unnecessary to have succession plans for every employee. There seems to be an HR fad to have personal development plans for each employee, known as PDPs. These become an administrative nightmare and I have yet to see anyone produce evidence that this produces any added value. On the contrary, the evidence leads to disappointment in employees when promises made are seldom met due to insufficient budget or training functions that just are not geared up for such a monumental task. If the Training development function wishes to pursue this, then proper succession planning particularly at a senior level needs to be done separately and with great rigor.

Second—there is little real evidence to support that performance appraisal is the most appropriate tool for selecting people who are suitable for the next levels. The appraisal sifts the average from the best, but this is in the current job with their current line manager who may have themselves little knowledge of the intellectual and interpersonal skills at higher levels in the organization and through no intentional fault may make recommendations based simply on the fact that they like the employee concerned.

Succession planning is therefore an essential part of any organization for continuity and consistent improvement of leadership at all levels. Failure to do this correctly can result in a dramatic reversal of an organization's fortunes (e.g., Marks and Spencer in the early 2000s).

Please be careful with succession planning—there are three compo-nents to the process and they are each performed by different part of NEW HR. This can be seen on the NEW HR functions chart featured in Chapter 1. (1.4) With every extra person dealing with a part of the process, there is a significant possibility of an increase of a mistake or lack of commitment to the final objective.

6.4.1 The Process and Choices Available

Throughout, we have agreed that a process approach to New Workforce Planning is the way ahead. Information and decisions based on fact and sound statistics rather than it's "my opinion" approach.

6.4.2 The Key Steps

1. Identification of the key, critical posts in the organization that must have a succession plan. These posts can be at any level in the orga-nization. The good news from a planning point of view is that these critical posts won't be that many.

2. Examine the incumbent, what predictions and forecasts can be made about when the post could become vacant—if there is a lack of predictable—then the scenario must be—at any time.

3. Ensure you have a consistent approach for selecting potential re-placement for these key positions. From experience, I am heavily in favor of heavy duty assessment centers either 1 or 2 days in duration. These need to be professionally run by a team of experts. Also, the bar needs to be set at the level the potential successors are likely to arrive at—this enables the training personnel to do a training needs assessment at a later date.

4. Which succession planning technique is appropriate for the job you are planning for? You have three choices, each of which is different, the final decision you will need to make on your organization, cul-ture, and expectations.

   a. *The Group approach.* This approach takes a group of employees all of whom will have been in the top of the assessment center process. The group is developed as a group and is then available to management as the pool of employees for future selection into a key post. Please do not get this confused with a low-level management development program. The program will produce a top quality group—with a strong sense of identity and very good interpersonal skills within that group, a strong core of high-level talent. The shortfall comes when the first vacancy occurs—who gets it? Managing this is like walking on broken glass and is the one shortfall this method has; if it's not managed properly then the cohort attrition can suddenly become high caused by their perceived expectations not being met.

b. *The external approach.* We have acknowledged that our focus is only on the critical key positions. Using a head-hunter approach, you simply find the best people in the market place who have a proven track record. This process ensures that you get the best of the best on an international platform. The major problem with this is that existing employees in the organization resent this often saying—"no matter how good you are they will always appoint from outside"—this is of course a massive demotivator. This can be resolved in some circumstances by having an assessment center with the external candidate(s) and some internal candidates— selection made on the best performance at the assessment center. If this cannot be done—then HRM needs to articulate clearly why an external candidate has been sought.

c. *The individual approach.* This is just what it says. We run an assessment center for all the people who are in contention for the key position. The best person will be selected and will then have a written contract to that effect. The person that came second in the assessment then becomes the standby, also having a contract to that effect. The person chosen then has their training needs identified by the current key post holder and a development plan is drawn up and executed. The current key post holder becomes a mentor to the successor, ensuring that they are ready for the post when it becomes vacant. When the new incumbent takes on the key position, sufficient work and development has taken place to make sure the transitioning take place smoothly and with the minimum of fuss. In due course, "the standby" then goes through the same process being mentored by the new incumbent to the job, thus building continuity.

6.4.3 The Roles of the Three Parts of HR

HRP—workforce planning—to identify the key positions

HRM—to carry out whatever assessments are needed and to agree with management the right person for the position. Also to draw up all the contracts needed

HRD—to carry out all the training development and mentor coordination as required to preset dates

6.5   Emergency Planning

Warning—don't wait until an emergency happens! Most companies have well-rehearsed emergency plans. They tend to cover software, hardware, buildings, plant, and equipment. Surprisingly and often, people are not included.

Looking at a couple of what-if scenarios:

What's the plan if an office block was destroyed by an earthquake and the majority of the staff were killed? Where do the people come from to run the business?

A major flooding incident wipes out a manufacturing plant—where do the people come from with the right skills, to get things back together again?

A plan needs to be drawn up by workforce planning to cover such remote situations.

Some of the workforce planning actions should be:

- Who are the people in the organization who can respond well to manage in a crisis?
- Where will additional manpower come from? A good source would be:
  a. The retired
  b. Women who have left to start a family

    c. Students from local universities—a pre-agreement would need to be in place

    d. The armed forces have a mass of experience (and equipment)—again, pre-agreements would need to be in place.

- The database needed to start the plan needs to be created and held in a number of off-site locations.

CHAPTER 7

Formulas and Unit Costs

Dr. Tony Miller's formulas for organisational efficiency – 2016/17

FORMULA 1. Pearsons moment correlation for two data comparisons eg. Age v productivity

FORMULA 2. Reliability (attendance) index

W × 9' × D – BI > software = R%

9' is the spell of absence
9' is the spell of absence
D is the duration of the absence
BI is the Bradford Index (as recorded)
R is the reliability score based on a 1-100 scale

FORMULA 3. LSI Labour stability index

FORMULA 4. Chi The cohort turnover index

FORMULA 5. ESUC. Unit cost for any employee per day (divide by 8 for hourly rate)

FORMULA 6 Competency averages

FORMULA 7 How much does appraisal cost

FORMULA A. 8 The value of re-engineering a process

FORMULA. 9 HR and training ROI

FORMULA 10 How many people do you need to run the organisation?

FORMULA 11 How many trainers do you need to deliver in-house training

FORMULA 12. Calculating prime working days PWD

© Tony Miller 2016/17

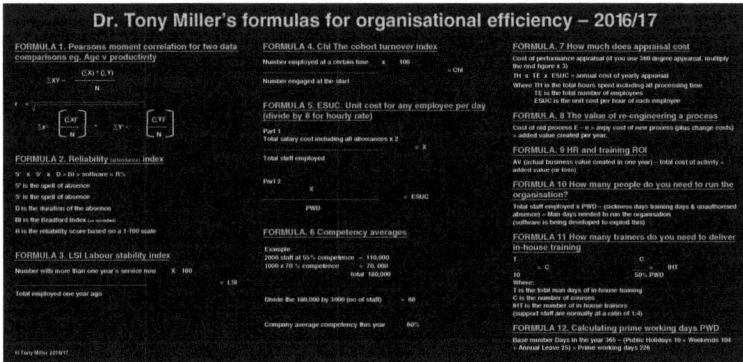

7.1   Days Worked—Prime Working Days
Formula 12 PWD

In nearly all workforce planning, work sooner or later you will need this calculation. How many days do people actually work in your organization; normal reply 365, but it's not true; so how many days do your human resource work. The calculation will vary from company to company; an acknowledged average is 226 days a year. When you use the formula, you will need to adjust the figures for an exact fit for your company.

Formula 12

> **Days in the year 365 − (Holidays 25 + Public Holidays 10 + Weekends 104) = 226 PWD**

The figure of 226 becomes the amount of days for productivity calculations, business expansion, or contraction calculations and the basis of calculating the employee standard unit cost (ESUC).

7.2   What Is the ESUC for Days Actually Worked?— Formula 5

The employee's standard unit cost is the basis of all calculations for efficiency, production costs, and efficiency savings. This is one very emotive figure, once you understand how it's calculated then run it past the finance Director to get the figure approved—remember, this is a rough unit cost, it's an average—not an exact figure. It's good enough for us to do a range of calculations and predictions.

7.2.1 A Worked Example of Formula 5

This is a company that employs 3,000 people with a total salary bill that includes salaries, overtime, car allowance, housing allowance, and ALL allowances including medical and any tax contributions. In this example, it amounts to £125,280,000.00.

You will see on the calculation that the total salary costs are multiplied by 2. Two is our real expenses we can attribute to every employee training, electricity, facilities, IT, floor space, company vehicles, etc.

If you have lots of spare time, you can work this out by looking at the annual accounts (private sector only), but for simplicity we use 2 as the factor. There are a few companies where the factor would be higher, such as in Google, Apple, Facebook, etc.

Remember, you are not the company mathematics department—you just need working standard figures.

We then divide the top-line total by the number of employees, which gives us X.

ESUC. To find the Unit cost for any employee per day		
Part 1		
Total salary + associated costs £125,280,000.00 × 2		
$\dfrac{\text{Total salary + associated costs £125,280,000.00} \times 2}{\text{No. of employees 3,000}}$	=£83,520	X

X is then divided by 226 (PWD) to give you the ESUC per day, which is the true cost of each employee in the organization.

$$\frac{X\ (\pounds 83{,}520)}{226} = \textbf{ESUC £369 divide by 8 (depending on Country)}$$
$$\textbf{to get hour rate £46}$$

Understanding these two formulas 5 and 12 enables you to take a hard look at what people do in the time they are actually available for work.

I have experienced little comment on calculating the PWD, but the ESUC always seems very controversial, often the comment from CFOs is that it not the way we do it—my reply is always the same to this statement— "well please show me the formula you use"—of course there is not one.

7.3   How Much Does Appraisal Cost—Formula 7

Performance appraisal is one of the most costly, time-intensive, and disliked processes inflicted by HR. Ask HR how much their process costs—don't hold your breath while waiting for the reply. The fact is that properly run performance appraisal is essential particularly for workforce planners. It gives us two of our three critical pieces of management information. Competency scores and performance scores. So, like it or hate it—we need it.

Cost of a performance appraisal for a normal (not 360) appraisal

$\textbf{TH} \times \textbf{TE} \times \textbf{ESUC} = \textbf{annual cost of yearly appraisal}$

Where TH is the total hours spent including all processing time
TE is the total number of employees
ESUC is the unit cost per hour of each employee
So let's examine the cost of appraisal for a company employing 5,000 people with an average employee unit cost of £46 per hour.

For each appraisal:
Appraiser's time preparing . 5 hours × £46   £23.00

Apraisee's time preparing . 5 hours × £46	£23.00
Appraisal time for appraiser 1 × £46	£46.00
Appraisal time appraisee 1 × £46	£46.00

After the appraisal—completing documentation appraise . 5 hours × £46 £23.00

After the appraisal—talking and reflecting appraise . 5 hours × £46 £23.00

HR processing time for each appraisal . 5 hours × £46	£23.00
Subtotal	£207.00
3,000 employees × £207	**£621,000.00**

In addition, it would be fair to add the cost of misdirected training identified from appraisal. This could be as high as 70 percent of the training budget—the cost of which would need to be added to the calculation.

In our example, we have a cost to the business of £621,000.00—to get just a simple return on investment, we need to get each year £621,000.00 of measurable bottom-line benefits. Can your appraisal system deliver this type of performance?

If you go beyond return on investment to seek added value, then it would be reasonable to expect to see a 20 percent added value each year. In other words, each year the system is in place, we should expect to see minimum measurable benefits of £745,200.00. Can your system deliver this type of business performance?

7.4   HR and Training ROI Formula 9

AV (actual business value created in 1 year) − total cost of activity = added value (or loss).

This is a very simple formula used to measure added value. It's particularly relevant to Workforce planners in the New Workforce planning arena as the value created is so high it would be the basis of making the department a profit center in its own right.

A very recent example would be the BMW case study shown in Chapter 6.

Value created 7% improvement in productivity + reduction in sickness − the process costs €50,000 = ROI added value

Due to confidentiality restrictions, regretfully I can't reveal to you the value of the two benefits in BMW, but as an example, these figures are very substantial and very significant.

7.5   How Many People Do You Need to Run the Organization? Formula 10

During the present world difficulties, the question most often asked by CEOs and CFOs is how many people do we really need to run the organization?

The question then that needs to be asked is "Is all of the planned work being completed?" The answer most of the time is a rather reluctant one—but it's yes in most cases. If that is so, then certain assumptions can be made and the following formula can be deployed to get a gauge for the right size needed for the organization.

Total staff employed × PWD − (training days & Reliability total days) = Man days needed to run the organization

The result is one of fact—that's how many man days were needed. There is no suggestion that people can't be off sick or that the training should stop, but the figure gives you a base line to work from.

In the Western world, during 2011 and 2012, in many organizations, right-sized reductions of 20 percent have been common with little if any detrimental effect to the function of the organization.

You can further refine the figures by looking at the percentage in the organization of poor and average performers. These examples are in Chapter 4 in the section on Performance.

A full step-by-step example of how to do this is from page 102.

7.6   Calculating Average Competency Levels—Formula 6

This is not really a significant formula, rather a straightforward mathematical calculation. It's in this section as it's the one calculation where most mistakes are made. The example just shows the mathematical process.

This calculation would be used for the three prime Productivity indicators, **Competency, Performance, and Reliability.**

Example:

2,000 staff at 55% competence = 110,000

1,000 × 70% competence = 70,000   total 180,000

Divide the 180,000 by 3,000 (no. of staff) = 60

Company average competency this year 60%

7.7   Missing Formulas

Lots—most don't work, many others have just been replaced with appropriate software packages. One of my favorite tools as a consultant is the one devised by the late Dr. Michael Hammer—F.A.C.E.

Is it Fast, is it Accurate, is it Cheap to use, is it Easy to use? This is a very useful concept to keep in your mind when being part of the New Workforce Planning. Focus on matters that will make a difference to organizational efficiency—get the big picture—keep focus at the strategic level—that's where the big gains are made.

CHAPTER 8

The New Productivity Dashboard

8.1 Background to the Dashboard Concept

The productivity dashboard is a significant leap ahead for HR and is far more in tune with what is done to produce real organizational results. The first move in this measurement many years ago was the Key performance indicators. They were a good start—bit just like competencies, the process rapidly got overcomplicated as various consultancy companies sought to "Sell" the system—warts and all. Working with key performance indicators can, if one is not careful, work against the total benefit to the organization.

Two examples where KPIs failed the organization:

8.1.1 Financial Services Company x

The Sales Director of this company that sold insurance had a KPI to increase sales by 6 percent in one calendar year.

The target was achieved—the Director got a substantial bonus. In the next year, the renewals fell by 10 percent—the people did not like the pressure selling that was taking place. There was a lack of joined-up thinking linking sales to retention although this was 2 years before this was picked up.

8.1.2 *Large Manufacturing Company*

> *Another example of where disconnected KPIs have an adverse effect on business performance. One of the KPI, of the training function was to complete 9 days of training, on average, for each employee and to spend on the agreed budget. In the same year, the operations function was targeted with improving output and reducing head count.*

> *In this company, operations did not release anyone for training to do their very demanding KPI—and but also fell short of their target*

> *Meanwhile, in the support functions of the business, many employees were forced into having 25 days' training—the training function met their KPI!*

If KPIs are used, their approach must be well orchestrated and a clear view of what the organization needs has to be made clear to everyone to avoid mismatches in effort.

Progressing forward, the best example of using this dashboard approach is Sysco. The value they are able to demonstrate on a year-by-year basis using this system is amazing.

The process has been refined and at the same time has retained its simplicity allowing organizations to take a do-it-yourself approach, setting their own target levels depending on the industry, country, and economic climate.

8.2   The Three Productivity Indicators

In the previous chapters, we have discussed Competency, Performance, and Reliability and know that we can measure all three. One of the great strengths of the performance dashboard is that it's put on display in each department, so you can see at a glance how you are doing throughout the year against the target scores or presets.

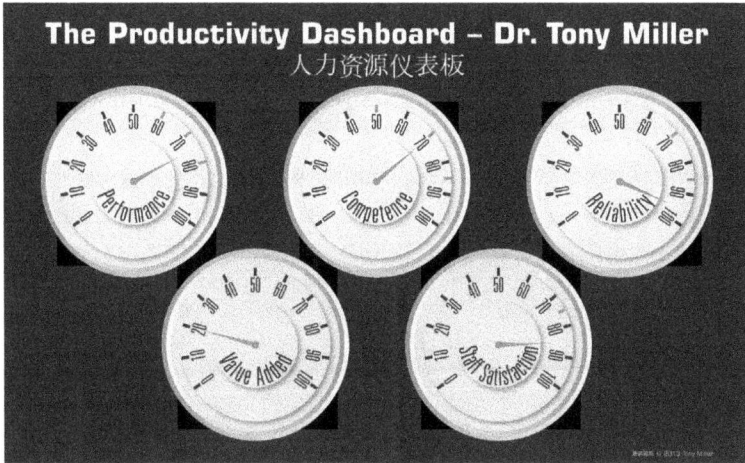

The Productivity Dashboard – Dr. Tony Miller

人力资源仪表板

Just to recap:

Competency gives the organization, quality, safety, and conformance to standards.

Performance gives volume, speed, output, low processing cost, and agility.

Reliability gives attendance, value, minimum head count, and dependability through stability.

These three measures give us that all-important productivity.

8.3   Staff Satisfaction

There is a lot of evidence to show that high levels of staff satisfaction reflect in low turnover, and often but not always, higher productivity.

Measuring staff satisfaction is therefore a critical factor in our dashboard.

A word of caution here—be careful not to be over-zealous and overdo it; once a year should be ample, less if you are in a period of rapid change.

Most organizations prefer to design their own surveys, make sure you are satisfied it will give you the evidence that you need and that the results are available on a 1-to-100 score as previously discussed. If you want to buy in a ready-made solution, you could use one of the more generic products such as the SHL corporate culture lite.

Once the survey has been completed over a number of years, you could start doing correlations with the survey results and see how they relate to the three productivity drivers, Competency, Performance, and Reliability.

It is unlikely that Workforce planning will be involved actually doing the surveys, but the scored results are a critical part of our data collection needed for various correlation exercises.

8.4   Added Value

What is added value? It's the value you can demonstrate above total cost.
We use **Formula 9 HR and training ROI**

AV (actual business value created in 1 year) − total cost of activity = added value (or loss).

Workforce planning is the perfect department for becoming an added value function, and therefore a profit center; closely followed we hope by the other parts of NEW HR.

The value is measured in 1 year so that it is directly linked to most organizations' budgetary cycle.

HR has to change due to two major influences, the changing quality of people and a growing need to measure human capital and to develop that capital into a measurable strategic business advantage. People are constantly improving, we have higher education standards, and greater literacy and a high level of competence with work-related IT. This makes today's employee vastly superior than at any other time in history. Today's employee therefore needs less management control and less process control to work effectively. Given that backdrop, it's essential that HR in all its facets alters to reflect these changes.

Businesses now want a human resource department that can add value. A profit center rather than a burdensome cost. Logically, if NEW HR is a major player in all things related to our greatest cost and asset—people—how could it possibly be a cost center?

The chart sets out to set the standard for the current financial year. In the example on the chart, we have the added value target preset at 20 percent.

If that preset was for the entire HR function, then the added value it would need to show would be a contribution in one financial year that was 20 percent over total cost. It's up to you to decide at what level you set the bar, start off at a manageable figure—say 5 percent and move upwards as you gain confidence and success.

In HR functions, workforce planning would be a good first choice to be moved to added value results. Linking the percentage of added value would be a sensible way of creating a bonus scheme for the workforce planning team.

8.5   Using the Dashboard to Fuel Bonus Systems

The Productivity indicators provide an input for your bonus scheme. Using the three presets:

Competency 70%

Performance 75%

Reliability 95%

With this input data, you can use a hopper-type system to feed a bonus scheme, either team based or individual based.

Hopper Bonus System

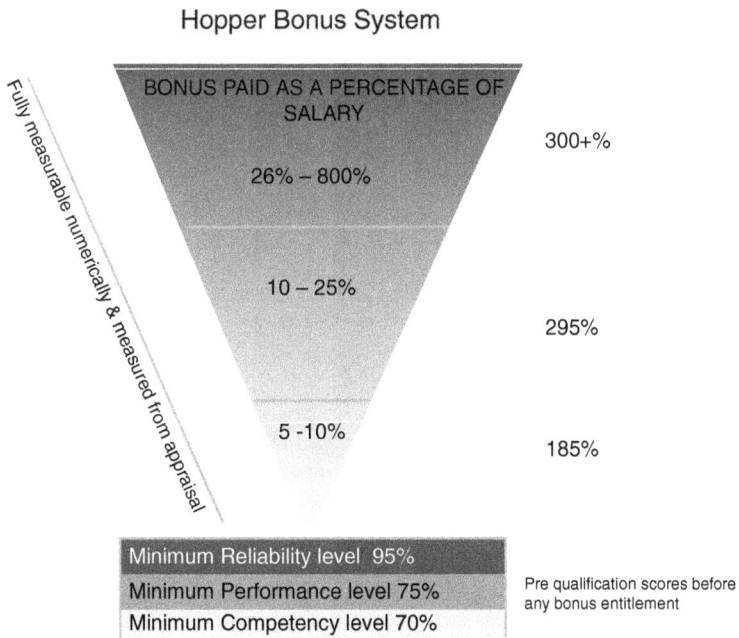

BONUS PAID AS A PERCENTAGE OF SALARY

Fully measurable numerically & measured from appraisal

26% – 800%   300+%

10 – 25%   295%

5 -10%   185%

Minimum Reliability level 95%
Minimum Performance level 75%   Pre qualification scores before any bonus entitlement
Minimum Competency level 70%

If you fail to meet any of the minimum scores, they are excluded from the scheme and any other enhancement to the basic salary/wage. This is a very fair and equitable way of putting a scheme together as the rules for entry are very clear. Earning bonus is then decided only on the performance scores as both competency and reliability are the minimum quality-assurance figures.

CHAPTER 9

Workflow Management/ Business Process Re-engineering

9.1   Introduction

There is a blurred line between the differences of these two activities. In short—

1. *Work flow management* can be done quickly, and usually involves minor and low-cost changes that improve workflow.
2. *New business process re-engineering* is really a complete and radical re-design of the entire process. It takes a long time to do and in most cases, the new process has no resemblance to the process it replaces.

9.2   Workflow Management in Action

In all the instances where significant improvement has been made in workflow management, the same criteria seem to have been present:

Urgent
Crisis
If we don't do something immediately—we will go bust

It may have been a coincidence; but this has happened so many times so—I don't think so. When I was working in America, I did many of these projects and found them all to be very successful in small and large companies alike.

The practical example I will show you here was with a large European manufacturing company. This example is now used in all our Workforce Planning Master Classes—as it has all of the data, figures, and issues in it.

9.2.1 The Case Study: Lane Engineering

9.2.2.1 The Background and Data

Lane is an Engineering Company, founded in 1860 by Everard Lane, an Engineer. The business went from father to son, and the company went public in 1991. The stock value had grown, very slowly and the shares were viewed as a safe but low-income choice by the city analysts.

Lane's product was spherical joints used in the gear linkages of certain sports cars. Its market had always been in Europe, and its product sold through one distributor whom the company had worked with since 1860.

Lane had only one competitor in its market, Squires Engineering, which had come into the market in late 2011.

This year, 2015, and it came as a complete surprise; Squires started selling the same product 8 percent cheaper than the Lane product. Quality appeared to be the same, and in the course of 9 months Lane have seen their market share evaporate, share value has plummeted, and things have become serious.

Engineering (Operations) are taking delivery of high-speed robotic lathes later this month, but in your discussions with the Managing Director you have been told to come up with a rethink on the entire way the organization trains and develops people. Things are tense in the company and it's been made clear to you if you don't come up with some solutions within the week, your successor will have the opportunity of doing better.

Some facts about the company and its structured and reward scheme:

- Lane employs 1,390 people all based on one factory site.
- The top-end structure consists of a managing director (Mr. Lane), five main board directors which are Support Services, Finance, Engineering Operations, Sales, and a Marketing Department. The key function is the Engineering

Operations that employs 1,143 people which includes the Director. This leaves 245 employees in the remaining functions.

- Engineering Operations is structured much as it was in 1950. A main board director, a senior engineer directly responsible for main production. This position, the senior engineer, has six managers and their six assistant managers reporting to him. Each of the assistant managers has seven supervisors reporting to them and each supervisor has one assistant supervisor reporting to them. Each supervisor and assistant supervisor jointly manages 14 people (these are the production workers). The second component of the Engineering Operations is another senior engineer who is responsible for finishing, packing, and distribution of the product. This senior Engineer has four managers, each of the managers has an assistant, and each assistant has seven supervisors reporting to him. Each of the seven supervisors has one assistant each. Each supervisor and assistant supervisor jointly manages 14 people.
- An organizational chart is not available as the HR Department has not yet produced one.
- 50 people have left Engineering Operations in the last year, 7 percent of those were over 55.
- Pay. Lane has always been a good employer in the area. The basic pay is rather high for the industry, but has kept a loyal and skilled workforce with unavoidable turnover less than 2 percent. There is not a bonus system as Mr. Lane does not like them as he is convinced quality will suffer.
- SUC is £46.00 per hour. Working hours are 8 am till 4 pm 5 days a week. Each worker gets 25 days holiday a year, employer matched pension contribution, private medical, free canteen, and a factory sports complex. There is an onsite nurse and dentist.
- In the factory, sickness runs at 8 percent, and lateness seems to be a problem.

- Most of the factory employees up to main board have progressed up through the organization—promotion probably based on time served.
- Most of the training provided seems to be done in-house and is focused on safety and specific factory skills.
- Five percent of the Engineering Operations workforce is 55 and over.
- Current production is 10,000 units per day all completed by the current day staff in a standard working day.
- Profit is 9 percent over cost.
- If Lane were to match Squires' price, the company would run at 1 percent profit.
- Lane have started losing good people to its main competitor.
- All of the staff have been with the company for over 2 years.
- Recent gossip around the company is that the company is in real financial trouble and as a result is likely to go bust.
- HR has reported getting in a huge number of requests for references.
- Mr. Lane has purchased five robotic lathes that can produce 2,000 units each in 8 hours. These are self-loading and completely automatic.
- Total salary budget is (for 3,000 employees) £125,000,000.

9.2.1.2 Restrictions

- The company is subject to international employment law.
- There is no possibility of significantly increasing the salary/remuneration budget.
- It is important that any proposals are introduced immediately as the financial situation is becoming serious.
- There has been significant activity on the trading of shares as investors have become nervous.
- Mr. Lane is very much against making anyone redundant.
- Mr. Lane has little respect for HR and their associated services as he feels the only "bread winner" is Engineering Operations.

Please note

The name and location of the company have been changed as this is a real case study in which we are involved.

9.2.1.3 The Workflow Requirement

The task is to organize the factory to be able to produce an additional 5,000 items in a 24-hour period—bringing the total factory output to 15,000 units.

- What would the best work balance be for two shifts using new robotic lathes which are to be used (night time only) with three staff to supervise per 8-hour night shift—these staff are to come from operations (workers).
- The factory will continue as normal during the daytime but the packaging department will have to deal with the manual packaging and distribution of 15,000 items a day.
- How would packing need to be structured (workers only) to achieve a workflow balance?
- What are the amendments needed in operations?
- What will the added value be—each unit's profit is £50.00.
- Cost of the robotic lathes (previously purchased) £4.7 million.

9.2.1.4 What Was Done

1. The problem with the workflow was going to be in the labor-intensive area of packing.
2. As the robotic lathes had more capacity than needed, it was this area where a balance in production could be made.
3. Critical area
   1. How much work was done by the packers, e.g., how much did the individual do each day? 392 workers—25.5 units each per day
   2. How much work did the production workers do? 588 workers— 17 units each per day

4. How many people were needed in packing to deal with an extra 5,000 units of production each day?

$$\frac{5,000}{22.5} = 196 \text{ extra people}$$

5. People needed from production to man the night shifts—6
6. 588 workers in production − (6 night shift + 196 people to production) = 386 people left in production with a loss of 386 × 17 production units a day = 6,562 lost production
7. Night shift work load 5,000 (new work) + 6,562 (lost day production) = 11,562

$$\frac{11,562}{2} = 5,781 \text{ per shift}$$

9.2.1.5 Cost

Robotic lathes £4,700,000

Training for operations people moving into packing

(£96 training day cost + (£46 per hour rate × 7 hours) × 196 people) − £19,138.00

Training for night shift. (½ training day £48 + (hour rate £46 × 3½ hours) × 6 = £449.00

One group of delegates in the Middle East at a Masterclass practising techniques

Consultants' fees £200,000

Extra packing line (existing equipment used)

Total cost £4,919,637.00

ROI calculation Formula 9

AV (actual business value created in 1 year) − total cost of activity = added value (or loss). Business value 5,000 number of new units × 226 days × £50 profit per unit = **£56,500,000.00 Business value £56,500,000.00 − cost £4,919,637.00 = AV £51,580,363.00**

9.3   New Business Process Re-engineering

The new way of doing business process

What is a business process?

What is business process re-engineering?

No matter how hard you work, if the process is faulty you will not achieve the productivity improvements expected. Poor processes waste time and effort and can be a huge demotivator for conscientious employees.

So what is a process? My good friend, the late Dr Michael Hammer, who was the world's leading authority on Business Process Re-engineering (BPR) described a process as a group of activities that together create value and provide a service to the customer. That customer can be internal or external—it does not matter.

It's not a single activity, it's not how hard or well you work–it's the combined effect and the end result that's important. Unlike a fine claret wine, processes do not improve with age.

Why do we need New BPR?

The problem many organizations have is that no one admits to owning processes—so they become organizational orphans, left to wander and dysfunction. There is no point in spending vast sums of money on training if the basic process is faulty. Working harder is not our prime objective, what we are going to achieve is working smarter by doing the work effectively

There are many ways you can carry out business process re-engineering. You can call in a consultant although this is very expensive and it's hard to find someone to take ownership when the consultant leaves: or an alternative is a DIY approach involving future owner or owners of the process. It is my view that as this is such a key process; the way of doing it and the areas to be selected fall to New Workforce Planning Departments. Likewise the added value created by changing process should also be credited to Workforce Planning. So how do you go about doing business process re-engineering?

The key to success is to draw the existing process exactly as it happens on a swim lane chart. The swim lane chart, normally drawn on several flip chart sheets, must accurately represent exactly what happens in the process with exact timings which show the elapsed time. The total of the elapsed time and more importantly the "picture of the process" and is our starting point for dramatic and radical change.

9.4   The BPS Process

Our process consists of five stages.

Stage 1:

Identify the process to be examined. Make sure you and whoever else needs to, knows the process well.

You need to know exactly where it starts and where the process ends.

Stage 2:

Measure and map the process.

Walk through the process at least twice.

Time and record exactly what happens.

How many people involved at each stage, how long it takes, transmission time, delay time. We use a series of symbols to make it clear what happens, the main ones are:

An arrow for direction or transmission.

A D for delay.

An inverted triangle for filing.

A square for checking.

A circle for actual work done.

Main symbols

▣	CHECK
⬤	ACTION
▽	FILE
D	DELAY
◀───	DIRECTION

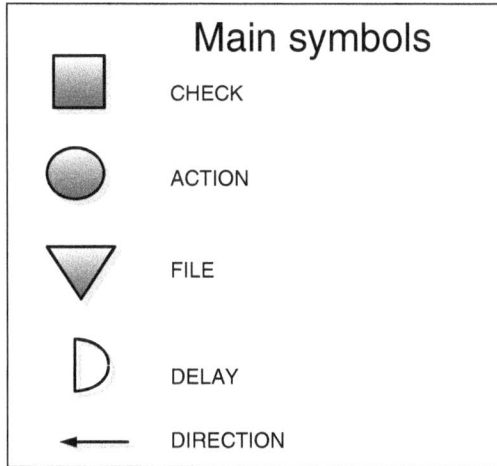

The picture you are building is of elapsed time.

This must be real and accurately measured. Elapsed time is exactly what it says.

If I put something in my out-tray for you at 5 pm in the afternoon and you look at it at 10 am the next day, the elapsed time is 17 hours.

When measuring what happens, remember that employees have breaks, lunch and have a start and finish time.

You are not attempting to find best performance in the process, merely record what happens on a day to day basis.

Mapping the process: in order that we and others fully understand the process, we need to map out exactly what we have recorded.

The maps we use are called swim lane maps.

These have the departments that are involved on the left with horizontal lines across the page segmenting the different departments.

As you draw the map, each step moves to the right, so that you can see the time line involved. Under no circumstances move to the left to conserve paper (you can't go back in time).

These maps need to be drawn up on large sheets of paper as you will want to review and amend them until you are sure they represent what typically happens.

Unsophisticated as it sounds, this is best done on the floor. We use symbols to make the mapping easier. Once finished, it looks rather

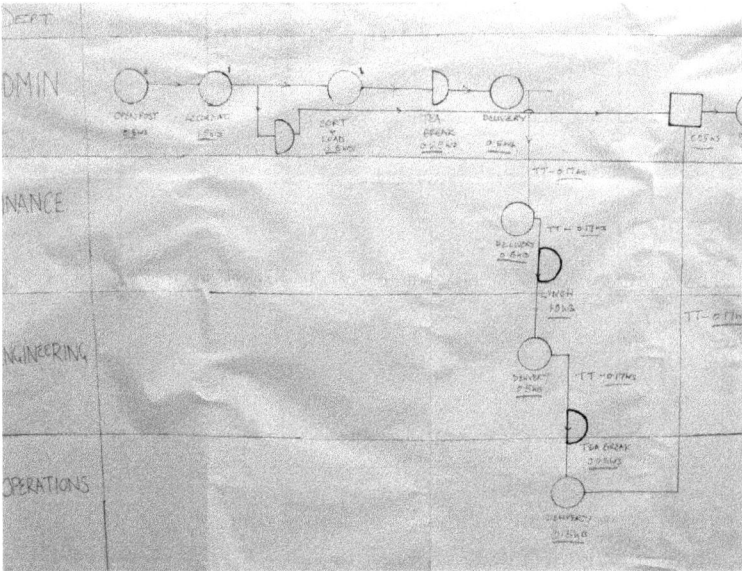

like a wiring diagram, but is very easy to follow and see the total steps in the process, together with delays, hand-offs, and excessive checking.

Adding up all the time then gives us the Elapsed Time for the process (ET). At this stage, there is little point in getting people to comment on the map as it's just a representation of what exists now.

If you are not familiar with the process, you could get a signature on the map to confirm that's what the current position is. At this stage be careful you don't give lots of ideas on how to make the process a bit better—that comes later.

There is an example for you to try, a simple example using the post-delivery for a small company, just to give you the opportunity to practice.

Stage 3:

Creativity and Innovation

Now, we have our process map we need to look at what we are going to do to improve the process. This is the first trap we come to. Doing this exercise is not about making an incremental improvement; it's about a complete redesign, starting from scratch—to make a dramatic improvement in process time and people efficiency. The late Dr. Michael Hammer, the American process re-engineering specialist, has a very good definition:

"The radical redesign of business processes for dramatic improvement"

The first word is "radical".

BPR gives us the opportunity to start with a clean sheet of paper. It give you the chance to start afresh, to create a process that has low overheads, is fast, accurate, cheap and easy to use (FACE)

The second word is "dramatic", BPR is not about a 5 percent change; it is about dramatic change where the new process is unlikely to have any resemblance to the existing process.

This is where you can create real added value for your company.

The difficulty that HR personnel will experience is that of neither being creative or innovative in their thinking.

Most people in today's HR are still very conservative in their approach to change. BPR requires a very bold and aggressive approach, which is often why consultants are used.

In the classic IBM finance study, they were able to take a 6-day process run by four people and reduce it to one person taking 4 hours.

That's both radical and dramatic.

Also, consider that the volume of business they were able to transact went up by a factor of 100.

Stage 4—the new process

Using your skills as discussed in step 3, re-draw the new BPR map. A tip here—when doing this, *do not look at your original ET map* or you will just end up modifying it and achieving only a small improvement in performance.

When you draw up this map, put the same departments in the swim Lane, and in the same order.

When you have finished your new map, put them both on the wall and you will see a real difference.

Stage 5—showing the ROI

FORMULA 8: The value of re-engineering a process

Cost of old process E − e = avpy cost of new process (plus change costs) = added value created per year.

9.5   Example for You to Try

Postal delivery process—M. Co. America

Post received 7.30 am in post room

Post opened approximately 250 items per day

Two people are involved in this operation which takes 30 minutes

All incoming items are recorded in a book—the book records the person who sent the correspondence, the company, the topic and who it's been assigned to. One person does this task and it takes 1½ hours.

Difficult items are sent to a Senior Manager who will do the allocation. This can take some time and if this happens, due to the delay, the item is normally put back into the system the next day for recording and then delivery.

When the post-delivery clerk arrives, he sorts the mail and loads the post trolley and commences the delivery of the mail. Sorting and loading take 1/2 hour.

Delivery of the mail by the Post-Delivery Clerk to the four offices. Calculate the time for pushing the trolley from department to department. Normally 10 minutes. Also, calculate how long it takes to sign in the book for each item received.

When the post clerk arrives back to the post room, someone later in the day checks the book to ensure all items of post have been signed for. If there are items where the recipient did not sign then the item is written in the book for delivery the next day. The postal clerk also writes a handwritten note explaining when the item was received and when it was attempted to be delivered.

Don't forget—the post room staff work 8 hours a day. They will have a 1-hour lunch break and tea/coffee breaks (15 minutes).

This process has been in operation for 10 years and everyone liked it.

Complete stages 1 and 2 and draw up a process map calculate the elapsed time (ET).

Example 12.2015

Administration including post room	
Finance	
Engineering	
Operations	

Results—see Appendix 2.

In Conclusion

New Workforce Planning has to be the most exciting place to be in HR. New approaches, software, and processes will make it unique as all its projections and recommendations are based not on some superficial fad but on sound data and processes.

Readers of this book are encouraged to download a variety of useful wall charts available from the website—free together with some complementary software.

On the topic of software, scheduling and rota applications have not been mentioned, but they are easily accessible and are all pretty standard, and used for hospital, hotel, and airline type applications. What is important is to explore the use of prediction and long-term forecasting—for it is in these areas where New Workforce Planning can really have a massive added value contribution.

When you examine the real value New Workforce Planning can bring to any organization—it's clear it should become a self-financing profit center. As mentioned in the foreword—the reward system for this department needs to be based on the added value created each year. After all, if HR can't maximize the potential of the organization's Human Capital, then what is its function and purpose?

Supporting this book is a complete consultancy service, in addition a number of lectures and masterclass workshops are run worldwide imparting the concepts, new change in direction and more importantly HOW TO DO IT. See the website www.tony-miller.com.

APPENDIX 1

Example 1: Data

Student:	Math (X):	Science (Y):	X^2	Y^2	X*Y
A	11	11	$11^2 =$	$11^2 =$	^
B	13	10	$13^2 =$	$10^2 =$	^
C	18	17	$18^2 =$	$17^2 =$	^
D	12	13	$12^2 =$	$13^2 =$	^
E	16	14	$16^2 =$	$14^2 =$	^
N =	$\Sigma X =$	$\Sigma Y =$	$\Sigma X^2 =$	$\Sigma Y^2 =$	$\Sigma XY =$

Have a go and see if you can do it!

Example 1: Complete Datatable

Student:	Math (X):	Science (Y):	X2	Y2	X*Y
A	11	11	$11^2 = 121$	$11^2 = 121$	11*11 = 121
B	13	10	$13^2 = 169$	$10^2 = 100$	13*10 = 130
C	18	17	$18^2 = 324$	$17^2 = 289$	18*17 = 306
D	12	13	$12^2 = 144$	$13^2 = 169$	12*13 = 156
E	16	14	$16^2 = 256$	$14^2 = 196$	16*14 = 224
N = 5	$\Sigma X = 70$	$\Sigma Y = 65$	$\Sigma X^2 = 1014$	$\Sigma Y^2 = 875$	$\Sigma XY = 937$

Hope you got it right!

Example 1: Equation

$$r = \frac{\sum XY - \frac{\left(\sum X\right) * \left(\sum Y\right)}{N}}{\sqrt{\left(\sum X^2 - \frac{\left(\sum X\right)^2}{N}\right) * \left(\sum Y^2 - \frac{\left(\sum Y\right)^2}{N}\right)}}$$

Put in the numbers.

Example 1: Step one—Put in the numbers

$$r = \frac{937 - \dfrac{(70) * (65)}{5}}{\sqrt{\left((70)^2\right) * \left((65)^2\right)}}$$

$$1014 - \text{------------}* 875 - \text{------------}$$
$$\qquad\quad 5 \qquad\qquad\qquad\qquad 5$$

Do the maths!

Example 1: Step two—Do the maths

$$r = \frac{937 - 910}{\sqrt{(1014 - 980) * (875 - 845)}}$$

Finish the calculation!

Example 1: Step three—Finish the calculation

$$r = \frac{27}{\sqrt{(34 * 30)}} \qquad\qquad r = \frac{27}{31.937438}$$

ANSWER: r = .854

r = .854 In other words, there is a strong positive correlation between the student's marks in maths and science. So what's the added value comment?

APPENDIX 2

Re-engineering

FORMULA 8. The value of re-engineering a process

Cost of old process E – e = avpy cost of new process (plus change costs) = added value created per year.

In the example given, the process time was 7.5 hours (that's just the elapsed time value)

7.5 hours $\times$ £46.00 $\times$ 226 = **E** £77,970

The best concept for this process

1 hour $\times$ £46 $\times$ 226 = **e £10,396**

Formula

E £77,970 – e £10,396 = £67,574 avpy (added value in 1 year)

APPENDIX 3

Organizational Maturity Questionnaire

This is an organizational forecasting model designed to be used for identifying when organizational change is needed. It's normally used in conjunction with the strategic model designed by Dr Tony Miller.

The factors considered in this instrument for rating the maturity of an organization are: THINKING FOCUS; WORKING PRACTICE; REWARD STRATEGY; TRAINING & DEVELOPMENT

You are asked to consider the individual behavioural indicators and descriptors within each column and decide which COLUMN of descriptors is most characteristic of your organization. You are likely to find that some descriptors from different columns apply to your organization but are asked to select the column that is most characteristic. You should rate this honestly and not respond with how you would like it to be, or how you think your organization should be.

Example

Thinking Focus

The focus of our organizational thinking can typically be characterized as:

Inventive—creating out of nothing	Increasing efficiency	Maintaining the status quo	Questioning the status quo—challenging every aspect of organizational life and activity
Discovery oriented—seeing what's possible	Establishing and consolidating know-how	Concern with increases in competition	Grasping the need for radical change
Risk-taking	Managing/minimizing risk	Managing costs out	Exploring opportunities to experiment and enter fields
Visionary—imagining what the organization could become	Targeting what needs to be achieved by the "end of the month"	Concern over declining profits	Establishing where to take risks
Future focused	Identifying opportunities for expansion	Potential "end of the line" for activities or products	
Targeted at exploring possibilities and ruling nothing out	Establishing and communicating organizational beliefs		

Thinking *Focus*

The focus of our organizational thinking can typically be characterized as:

Inventive—creating out of nothing	Increasing efficiency	Maintaining the status quo	Questioning the status quo
Discovery oriented—seeing what's possible	Establishing and consolidating know-how	Concern with increases in competition	Grasping the need for radical change
Risk-taking	Managing/minimizing risk	Managing costs out	Exploring opportunities to experiment
Visionary—imagining what the organization could become	Targeting what needs to be achieved by the "end of the month"	Concern over declining profits	Establishing where to take risks
Future focused	Identifying opportunities for expansion	Potential "end of the line" for activities or products	
Targeted at exploring possibilities and ruling nothing out	Establishing and communicating organizational beliefs		
☐	☐	☐	☐

Working Practice

Our approach to work may typically be characterized as:

Highly energetic	Long hours	Life balance issues	Re-energizing
Targeted at creating a future	Managed for efficiency	Functional focus	Breaking down barriers
Committed to developing key stakeholders	Prioritizing to meet key stakeholder needs	Focus on meeting stockholder needs	Focus on re-vitalizing existing or finding new stakeholders
Entrepreneurial	Setting up processes and systems	Maintaining processes	Recreating the organization
Offering high levels of independence and autonomy	Adoption of common standards	Reinforcing lines of management	Encouraging and facilitating entrepreneurial style where this hasn't existed
Guided by visionary leadership	Formalization of management practice	Initiatives focus on cost cutting and rationalization	Focusing on what really works and should be pursued
	Focused on improving market position	Focus on holding market position or managing its potential or actual decline	

Reward Strategy

Our reward strategy may typically be characterized as:

No formal pay scales	Grading and pay structures in place	Frequent reviews of pay levels	Questioning of reward practices
Fluid boundaries between jobs; no job evaluation system	Formal job evaluation process	Job evaluation works to reinforce established structure	Shift to de-layering and use of broad band classification of roles by competence
Pay above market rate to attract talent	Market rates monitored systematically using survey data	Benefits allocated hierarchically	Benefits replaced by straight cash
Rewards or bonus for performance are completely discretionary	Performance-related rewards formalized	Bonus reward strategy regarded as "timid"	Rewards for demonstrated added value only
Pay decisions are made by a few individuals at the top	Pay decisions centrally controlled with some discretion devolved	Moves to curb manipulation of appraisal/reward mechanism required	Focus shift to broad trends and "hot spots"
Sick pay and/or overtime is considered in an ad hoc fashion	Benefits packages devised for cost effectiveness	Increments seen as service related	
☐	☐	☐	☐

Training & Development

Our approach to training and development may typically be characterized as:

Individuals develop through experience in the job	Formal training provided	Training and development events granted as reward for performance not to enhance it	Concerted effort to create a "learning organization" maximizing learning from all quarters
Trial and error abounds	Development is guided by practices such as performance appraisal	Viewed as a cost that can be cut	Strategic perspective adopted to identify what training and development can add most critically
No formal training strategy	Training and development is udgeted for systematically	Courses and events have become institutionalized and remain on the curriculum irrespective of relevance	Transition management and change orientation feature heavily
Reactive; people learn in order to get the job done	Strong technical orientation in training provision		
Requirement to "hit the ground running"	Managerial training and leadership development appear on the curriculum		

Organizational Maturity Questionnaire Scoring Guide

Transcribe your scores for each section into the corresponding boxes below and add up the number of ticks in each column

Thinking Focus

☐   ☐   ☐   ☐

Working Practice

☐   ☐   ☐   ☐

Reward Strategy

☐   ☐   ☐   ☐

Training & Development

☐   ☐   ☐   ☐

Total

☐   ☐   ☐   ☐

The largest total indicates the most characteristic column for your organization.

Your average score will give you a position on the organization maturity grid—use the descriptors as shown below:

☐   ☐   ☐   ☐

Phase One   Early Phase Two   Late Phase Two   Phase Three

Organizational Maturity Chart

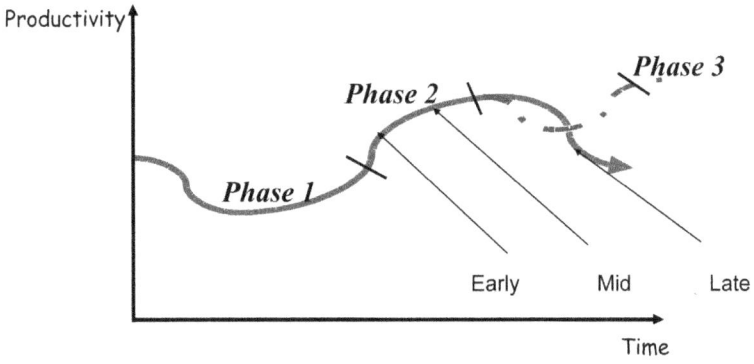

Copyright Tony Miller and Bill Best 2004

How to Rightsize any Organization—the Mathematics Involved

Step One

In the organization we are using for an example (a real organization in Europe), we have 3,000 employees. All the work is done each year—so how many hours are worked?

Most CEOs and CFOs will come up with the same answer.

Working hours per week 40 × weeks in a year 52 × Number of workers 3,000 = 6,240,000 **hours**

So, we have an assumption that all the work is being done by our 3,000 employees and we pay for and it takes 6,240,000 hours.

Step Two

To get a more accurate figure, we know (page 69) that we need to calculate work done by using Prime Working Days formula PWD.

PWD 226 days × Hours worked per day 8 hours × Number of employees 3,000 = **5,424,000 hours** actually worked. A big difference from our original assumption.

Step Three

As in all organizations, there are other lost time variables. In our test company, we find for each employee:

Average time lost through sickness	10 days per year
Average unauthorized absence	5 days per year
Average for Training/conferences	12 days per year
TOTAL extra time lost	**27 days per year per person**

Revised PWD 226 − 27 days = 199 days

Actual hours worked in our company

Days 199 X Hours per day 8 × employees 3,000 = 4,776,000 hours

Step Four

As we know, employees are in three categories—poor performers, average performers, and talented. We also know from a large survey done in 2015 how much work they do.

In our organization

17% are talented total 510—they work 6.4 hours a day

61% are average performers, total 1,830—they work 4 hours a day

22% are poor performers total 660—they work 1 hour a day

It is critical for all workforce planning predictive calculations that you know in your organization the percentages of works in the three categories and how many hours they actually work in a day.

Talented PWD 199 × hours worked per day 6.4 × number of employees 510 = total hours worked 649,536

Average PWD 199 × hours worked per day 4 × number of employees 1,830 = total hours worked 1,456,680

Poor performers PWD 199 × hours worked per day 1 × number of employees 660 = total hours worked 1,31,340

Total hours worked per year 649,536 + 1,456,680 + 131,340 = **2237556 Hours**

Step Five

We now know all the work done in our organization was done by 3,000 employees actually working **2,237,556 hours** although we are paying them for **6,240,000 hours.**

The question the management team must address is exactly how many hours a day do you expect your employees to work. In our company, it was decided that all employees should work 7 hours a day.

Therefore, if PWD is 226, the final calculation would be:

$$\frac{2,237,556}{1,582} = \textbf{1,414 rightsized figure. Actual number currently employed 3,000}$$

In this exercise, we have established that our company can be run using a total of 1,414 employees—this is an absolute minimum. In reality, just over 2,000 people rather than the 3,000 ran the company on the establishment.

A) 226 Prime working days $\times$ 7 hours a day = Hours each employee is expected to work each year **1,582.**
B) Now, we are going to divide our hours per year for each employee into our actual total hours worked to give the number of employees needed to run our company.

The thirteenth book from this
seasoned international author.
Another innovative
and essential read.

This book will be remembered as
one of the catalysts for HR Analytics and the creation of new workforce
planning. CEOs would be well advised to
take strategic and financial
advantage by using some of
the practices mentioned.

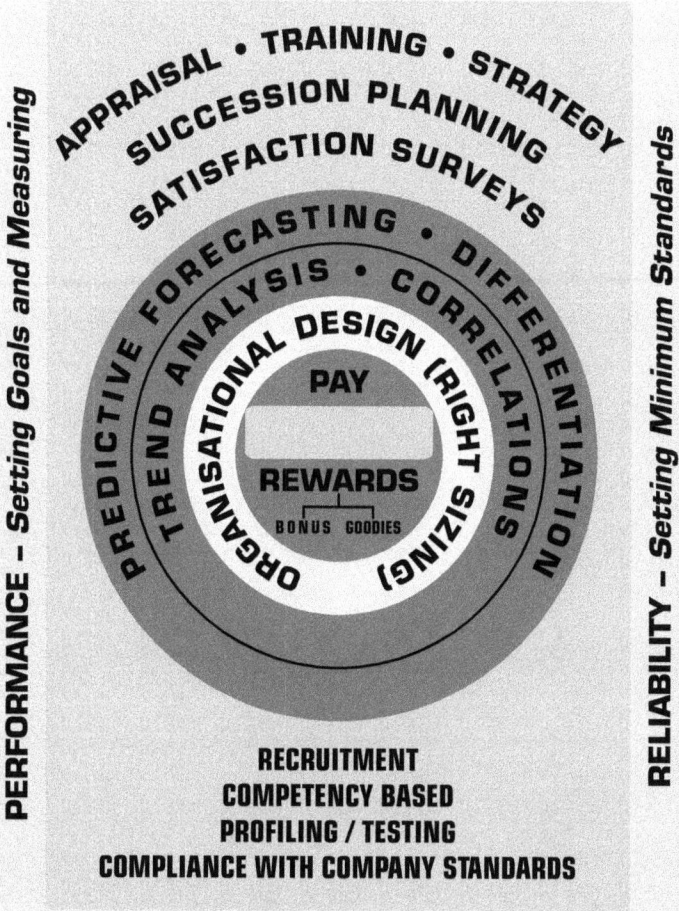

COMPETENCY – Setting Standards

APPRAISAL • TRAINING • STRATEGY
SUCCESSION PLANNING
SATISFACTION SURVEYS

PREDICTIVE FORECASTING • DIFFERENTIATION
TREND ANALYSIS • CORRELATIONS
ORGANISATIONAL DESIGN (RIGHT SIZING)

PAY

REWARDS
BONUS   GOODIES

PERFORMANCE – Setting Goals and Measuring

RELIABILITY – Setting Minimum Standards

RECRUITMENT
COMPETENCY BASED
PROFILING / TESTING
COMPLIANCE WITH COMPANY STANDARDS

Bibliography

Riggs, J.L. 1987.*Production Systems: Planning, Analysis & Control.* 4th ed. New York: John Wiley & Sons.

Zwillinger, D. 2012. *CRC Standard Mathematical Tables and Formulae.* Boca Raton: CRC Press.

Coolican H. 2004. *Research Methods and Statistics in Psychology.* 4th ed. London: Hodder & Stoughton.

Kim W.C. and R. Mauborgne. 2015. *Blue Ocean Strategy: How to Create Uncontested Market Space and Market the Competition Irrelevant.* Moston: Harvard Business Scholl Publishing.

Hesselbein F. and R. Johnston. 2002. *On High Performance Organisations.* San Francisco: Jossey-Bass.

Miller T. *New HR* 2012 - Management Performance Solutions Ltd Chelmsford UKFurnham, A. 2005. *The Psychology of Behaviour at Work: The Individual in the Organization.* East Sussex: Psychology Press.

Miller, T. – The Need for Process HR Re-engineering – Croners Publications issue 10-series Developing HR Strategy

Bartholomew, D.J. and A.F. Forbes. 1979. *Statistical Techniques for Manpower Planning.*2nd ed. Chichester: John Wiley & Sons.

Charan, R. – Know How

Miller, T. – The HR Dashboard – Croners 2011

Hiam, A. 1991. *The Vest-Pocket CEO: Decision Making Tools for Executives.* Englewood Cliffs: Prentice Hall Press.

Welch, J. and S. Welch. 2005. *Winning: The Ultimate Business How-to Book.* New York: HarperCollins Publishers.

Porter M and others – Harvard Business Review on Advances in Strategy 2002. Harvard Business School PressFurnham, A. and T. Miller. 2012. Demographic and Individual Correlates of Self-rated Competency. *SAGE Journal* 31, no. 3, pp. 247–265.

Dell M. 2006 Direct from Dell, Strategies that revolutionized an Industry. Collins Business essentialsAuletta, K. 2009. *Googled: The End of the World as We Know It.* New York: Penguin Books.

Diamond Docs and I Line entertainment – The real revolutionaries – 2010 – Video featuring William Shockley .Miller, T. 2016. *Successful Interviewing: A Concise Practical Process Approach.* Chelmsford: Management Performance Solutions.

Index

OTHER TITLES IN THE HUMAN RESOURCE MANAGEMENT AND ORGANIZATIONAL BEHAVIOR COLLECTION

- *The Illusion of Inclusion: Global Inclusion, Unconscious Bias, and the Bottom Line* by Helen Turnbull
- *On All Cylinders: The Entrepreneur's Handbook* by Ron Robinson
- *The Resilience Advantage: Stop Managing Stress and Find Your Resilience* by Richard S. Citrin and Alan Weiss
- *Marketing Your Value: 9 Steps to Navigate Your Career* by Michael Edmondson
- *Success: Theory and Practice* by Michael Edmondson
- *Leading The Positive Organization: Actions, Tools, and Processes* by Thomas N. Duening, Donald G. Gardner, Dustin Bluhm, Andrew J. Czaplewski, and Thomas Martin Key
- *Performance Leadership* by Karen Moustafa Leonard and Fatma Pakdil
- *The New Leader: Harnessing The Power of Creativity to Produce Change* by Renee Kosiarek
- *Employee LEAPS: Leveraging Engagement by Applying Positive Strategies* by Kevin E. Phillips
- *Making HR Technology Decisions: A Strategic Perspective* by Janet H. Marler
- *Feet to the Fire: How to Exemplify and Create the Accountability that Creates Great Companies* by Lorraine Moore
- *Successful Interviewing: A Talent-Focused Approach to Successful Recruitment and Selection* by Tony Miller

Announcing the Business Expert Press Digital Library

Concise e-books business students need for classroom and research

This book can also be purchased in an e-book collection by your library as

- *a one-time purchase,*
- *that is owned forever,*
- *allows for simultaneous readers,*
- *has no restrictions on printing, and*
- *can be downloaded as PDFs from within the library community.*

Our digital library collections are a great solution to beat the rising cost of textbooks. E-books can be loaded into their course management systems or onto students' e-book readers. The Business **Expert Press digital** libraries are very affordable, with no obligation to buy in future years. For more information, please visit **www.businessexpertpress.com/librarians**. To set up a trial in the United States, please email **sales@businessexpertpress.com**.

www.ingramcontent.com/pod-product-compliance
Lightning Source LLC
Chambersburg PA
CBHW071909200326
41519CB00016B/4550